☑ **W9-DBE-864**

**DATE DUE**

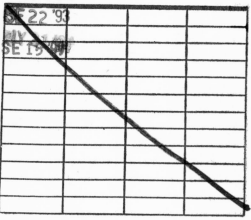

# Governance

## GOVERNANCE I
## The Presidency
## and the
## Constitutional System

Edited by
# Kenneth W. Thompson

Lanham • New York • London

Copyright © 1989 by the

White Burkett Miller Center of Public Affairs,
University of Virginia

University Press of America®, Inc.

4720 Boston Way
Lanham, MD 20706

3 Henrietta Street
London WC2E 8LU England

British Cataloging in Publication Information Available

Library of Congress Cataloging-in-Publication Data

Governance 1 : The Presidency and the constitutional system /
    edited by Kenneth W. Thompson.
        p.      cm. — (Governance ; 1)
    1. Presidents—United States.   2. Separation of powers—United States.
I. Thompson, Kenneth W.   II. Series: Governance (Charlottesville, Va.) ; 1.
    JK518.P725      1989      353.03'13—dc20      89–14622 CIP

ISBN 0–8191–7500–5
ISBN 0–8191–7501–3 (pbk.)

The views expressed by the author(s) of this publication do not necessarily
represent the opinions of the Miller Center. We hold to Jefferson's dictum that:
"Truth is the proper and sufficient antagonist to error, and has nothing
to fear from the conflict, unless by human interposition, disarmed
of her natural weapons, free argument and debate."

Co-published by arrangement with
The White Burkett Miller Center of Public Affairs,
University of Virginia

*To the animator*

*of discussions*

*on governance*

*at the Miller Center:*

*J. WILSON NEWMAN*

# Table of Contents

# Table of Contents

# Preface

This is a volume on governance, the first in a series that it is hoped will reawaken interest in the interconnectedness of the functions of the American political system.

For the first decade of its history, the Miller Center of Public Affairs dealt exclusively with the American presidency. In doing so, it sought to differentiate its program from other institutes and think tanks whose agenda covered a wide spectrum of policy problems from agriculture to zoning problems and spanning national, state and local settings. Critics question the dispersion of focus and efforts in many of these programs.

Indisputably, those who have been part of the Center's history have come to see the wisdom of focus on the presidency. It is oftentimes said that in research as in baseball, one scores runs by bunching hits. Surely, the fact that the Center has kept its eye on a single target, although admittedly a broad one, has led us to a concentration rather than a dispersion of effort. Because we have had a primary area of concern, our studies have been cumulative and reinforcing.

Along with satisfaction, we have also felt a certain unease that our institutional focus might be narrowing the scope of inquiry at times and in ways that obscured the fullest possible understanding of the presidency. Any schoolboy introduced to the Constitution observes that Articles 1, 2 and 3 provide for not one but three branches of government. The effectiveness of the presidency depends on relations with the Congress. The courts affect decisions of the executive and legislative branches especially as reflected in the Supreme Court's power of judicial review. Each branch affects the other and the strength of one depends on the harmonization of its efforts with those of the others. Chief Justice Warren observed that if each branch of the federal government were to pursue its own constitutional powers to the end of the trail, our system simply could not function. In Dean Rusk's words" "it would freeze up like an engine without oil." Comity and cooperation are imperative.

Therefore, to understand the presidency, it is essential to understand more than the presidency. The same is true of understanding the Congress or the Supreme Court. Each is part of the constitutional system as a whole and depends for its success or failure on the relationship of the parts with the whole.

Governance I is a first preliminary and tentative foray into studying interrelatedness within the constitutional system. It seeks particularly to relate the presidency to the rest of the system. Each contributor views the presidency not in isolation but as influenced by and influencing the Congress, the courts or administrative management within the political system. It is fair to ask if this approach provides a better measure of the workings of the executive than an analysis of the presidency set apart.

The answer to this question will depend on a series of inquiries being undertaken. We expect to continue what we have begun in Governance I in volumes that will follow. Having repeated our inquiries, we shall then pause for stock taking in assessing the utility and value of the governance approach.

# Introduction

Senator Charles McC. Mathias throughout a long and illustrious congressional career has demonstrated repeatedly the courage to take a fresh look at recurrent problems. With the growing national debt and an alarming if improving trade deficit, the need for such thinking is once more apparent. Senator Mathias does so in the first essay suggesting that nations still require a certain measure of independence in dealing with the rest of the world. At the same time, he acknowledges the realities of global interdependence. A two-tiered approach is needed to recognize the two dimensions. To confront such problems, elected officials must themselves have the support of the people to take unpopular stands that may require personal sacrifices. The problem of governance with respect to urgent problems is linked, therefore, with public participation in the electoral process and the relation of leaders to the public. Americans need to look again at the way we nominate our presidents. Senator Mathias makes a series of proposals for electoral reform drawing on his own political imagination and that of former Senator Howard Baker.

Congressman Richard Bolling evaluates the last five presidents measured against the standard of the American system of governance as a whole. Rather than considering presidents solely in terms of their skills as communicators or their competence as administrators, Bolling assesses them against their relationships with other branches of government and especially the Congress. In that connection, he asks specifically why they succeeded or failed. Some of his conclusions depart from conventional wisdom regarding the five presidents. In adopting the governance mode of analysis, Bolling helps us to understand the interdependency of the governing units in the American constitutional system and the extent to which a successful or a failed presidency depends on effective working relationships.

Jeffrey Bergner's chapter is a companion piece to Richard Bolling's. However, Bergner reflects on the relationship between the presidency and Congress from the viewpoint of changes in Congress, while Bolling maintains a focus primarily on the presidency. For his approach, Jeffrey Bergner is uniquely qualified having served as staff director of the Foreign Relations Committee, and before that, as Senator Richard Lugar's chief of staff. He reviews the dispersion of power for foreign affairs in the Congress and an accompanying dispersion within the executive branch involving such diverse bureaucracies as Agriculture, Treasury and Commerce. Bergner places considerable emphasis on the changes in party views of such issues as internationalism and free trade. He also notes a changing profile for the legislature with more independence from the political parties and any particular leadership group. Legislators are increasingly independent in their patterns of action.

Governance also involves the relationships between courts and the presidency. No one is better qualified to treat this subject than the great Virginian, former Justice of the Supreme Court Lewis F. Powell. The interconnections between the presidency and the Supreme Court are many and varied, but none has more importance than the president's role in nominating persons to serve on federal courts and in particular the U.S. Supreme Court. Approximately 20 percent of the persons nominated for Supreme Court have been rejected by the Senate. A study of this important presidential function seems crucial to a better understanding of the process of governance. However, Justice Powell examines other aspects of the work of the courts that influence governance in his "conversation at Monticello."

Judge Griffin Bell, who was attorney general in the Carter administration, examines judicial selection across an even broader sector of the American system of governance. For example, he reviews the appointment of U.S. attorneys arguing that their choice should be a matter for the attorney general, at least in the first instance. He considers a wide range of legal and constitutional questions and distinguishes between political and judicial issues. Judge Bell's and Justice Powell's chapters can usefully be read in conjunction with one another. They enhance our understanding of the wide ranging relationship between judicial and executive or legislative aspects of governance.

Edgar B. Young next discusses "Public Personnel and the Bureau of the Budget After the Brownlow Report." Mr. Young was present at the creation of the Bureau of the Budget and observed its growth and that of other agencies for reenforcing administrative management within the Executive Office of the President. Young throws a spotlight on the development of personnel selection processes within the executive branch and its relationship to political appointments by a new administration. Administration remains a basic aspect of governance and the interrelationships between a well-qualified career service and high level non-career appointees is crucial to the workings of a successful administration.

Professor Cecil V. Crabb, Jr. is the author of the concluding chapter in this volume on governance: "One Secretary of State at a Time: Avoiding Another Irangate." Specifically, his essay is an inquiry into the nature of governance in foreign policy-making and policy implementation. Crabb reviews the traditional role of the president and secretary of state in foreign policy but gives primary attention to the assistant for national security affairs. He offers a fivefold classification of the assistant in five distinct periods of American history arguing that in the Truman administration, the assistant to the president can be conceived of as "clerk," under Eisenhower as "coordinator," in the Kennedy-Johnson era as "policy advocate," in the Nixon-Kissinger years as "agent" paralleling if not surpassing Cabinet members in importance and under Reagan as illustrating "the insurgency model" leading to Irangate. As with the six previous contributors, Crabb helps us to understand governance by studying not only one official but old and new offices concerned with foreign policy and their interrelationships.

# I. Independence, Interdependence, and the Electoral Process

## SENATOR CHARLES McC. MATHIAS, JR.

**MR. EDGAR SHANNON, JR.:** It is my pleasure to welcome you to Monticello for a conversation with Senator Charles Mathias. We are delighted to have the senator with us for one of our series of conversations co-sponsored by the Thomas Jefferson Memorial Foundation and the Miller Center of Public Affairs. We are also pleased to have you, the audience, here to make conversation with our distinguished guest. It seems highly appropriate that we should assemble to talk about the presidency here in this house with the spirit of Mr. Jefferson looking over us. I'd like to introduce the director of the Miller Center, Ken Thompson, who will introduce our speaker.

**NARRATOR:** One of the challenges of organizing any kind of commission, such as the one which the Miller Center recently sponsored on presidential transitions, is to seek a current or retired legislator to be a leading member of the commission. The experience of the Miller Center may be similar to the experience of a number of other commissions. Whenever you begin discussing names under the category of legislative leaders, the name of Senator Mathias always comes to the fore. Even in his so-called retirement, he has not had the privilege of the kind of lonely isolation that Dean Rusk once remarked about, maybe in this very room, when he said, "The most difficult part of retirement is that when you are having dinner or lunch, no one any longer

1

comes over to your table and asks your views about U.S. foreign policy."

Senator Mathias was a United States Senator from 1969 until 1987. Before that, he served four terms as Congressman from the 6th District of Maryland. He was born in Frederick, Maryland, and was educated at Haverford College, Yale, and the University of Maryland Law School. He was admitted to practice and the Maryland bar in 1949 and to appear as counsel before the U.S. Supreme Court in 1954. He has served in many capacities in his public career, and it is significant that in every one of them, he seems always to have been called on to assume the next higher responsibility. For example, he started as seaman in the Navy and ended up as captain. It is a great privilege to introduce the senator.

**SENATOR MATHIAS:** Thank you, Ken. I appreciate very much the opportunity to come to Monticello today and have this conversation with you. I assure you that it will be a conversation and not a speech. Ken was very generous in his introduction, but he omitted one fact about my life of which I am very proud, and that is that I have a son who is a graduate of the Law School at the University of Virginia.

Your mention of Dean Rusk's description of lonely isolation calls to mind a conversation I had with Howard Baker shortly after he left the Senate. He said, "Do you know when I really knew that I was no longer a member of the United States Senate?" I said, "Howard, when was that?" He replied, "When I went to lunch and nobody else picked up the check."

One of the things, if not *the* thing, that made Thomas Jefferson proud was the fact that he was the author of the Declaration of Independence. That was certainly the one achievement in a life full of achievements that he liked to remember. And so it seems to me that it might be useful today if we could talk together a little bit about, not the Declaration of Independence, but the fact of independence itself. What is independence in the latter part of the twentieth century? What kind of dangers threaten our independence in the latter part of the twentieth century?

2

Is Thomas Jefferson's achievement of bringing about independence in any way at risk in our generation?

I suggest that we talk about this today, not merely because we are meeting at Monticello with the shadow of Jefferson looking on, but because we are in the middle of a presidential election campaign [1988]. It seems to me one of the useful things about presidential election campaigns is that they can direct our minds to the important issues that must be resolved in the years following the campaign. So it is with this practical purpose as well as the sentimental purpose that I raise the subject of the independence of the United States of America.

We are in debt. Debt for a nation is not always a bad thing. If one may quote Alexander Hamilton in this house, he once said that national debt may be a blessing if it is not too large. Our national debt is now well over a trillion dollars, an unbelievably large sum of money. I remember the days when people used to try to conceptualize a billion dollars, and they'd do so by comparing stacks of a billion dollar bills with the Washington Monument and things of that sort. But I don't know anybody who has tried to physically conceptualize a trillion dollars. It is an almost theoretical sum except for the fact that we have to pay interest on it. Forget for the moment ever paying it back and just think about paying interest on it. The interest is now beginning to amount to a significant portion of our national revenues. It will soon move through a quarter and up to nearly a third of our revenues. What this does is reduce the amount of discretion of the next president of the United States in allocating the resources of the nation to meet the needs of the nation. Our massive debt limits the judgment that the president may use in determining where resources should be applied. Of course if you add to the debt service the other fixed items in the national budget, the president's judgment becomes very limited.

I won't focus on that part of our dilemma this afternoon. Rather, I'd like to focus on the relationship that our debt has with other nations and with creditors in other nations because in the 1980s, the most important thing that has happened, I believe, is that the United States has moved from being the world's largest creditor to the world's

3

largest debtor nation. We do not have the resources in this country to fund our own budget deficit.

One of the reasons we don't, just in passing, is that we have such a low level of savings in this country. Benjamin Franklin's old rules of thrift seem to have gone out the window, and our savings rate is now between 2.5 and 3 percent, which is one of the lower savings rates in the world. It compares very poorly with that of the Germans or the Japanese, and even with that of the Russians. Since we don't form a sufficient pool of capital in our own country from which the government can borrow to meet its deficits, the government has had to go overseas to borrow.

In the 1980s virtually the whole of our government's overseas borrowing came not from private investors but from central banks—the official government banks of foreign countries, most notably the Central Bank of Japan. We anticipate that all foreign borrowing, within the relatively near future, will amount to as much as the national debt is today, and the national debt, of course, will continue to grow. Foreign debt will soon be something on the order of a trillion dollars by itself, a very alarming figure. Debt earns interest for creditors, so we will be sending roughly $50 billion out of this country every year just to finance our debt. I might add that in addition to the debt, which is projected for one trillion dollars, foreign investors have about $1.5 trillion invested in the American economy. So we have a $1 trillion debt on top of the $1.5 trillion of foreign investment in the dollar economy.

All of this is like Hilaire Belloc's description of the water beetle. He said the water beetle sped across the water's face with speed, dexterity, and grace. But if it ever stopped to think how it did it, it would sink. As long as all of this keeps going it seems to work, but if it ever slows down for any reason, if it ever stops . . . One of the reasons it hasn't slowed down is that the rate of return in this country has been relatively high; the dollar has been relatively stable because, above all, the United States has been a safe haven for money. I once asked a banker in Paris why the French loaned so much money to the United States, and he said, "What else would we do with it?" So the opportunities are limited in other parts of the world. But these are all relative factors, relative conditions, and they are subject to change. If the interest rate falters, or if the dollar value on exchange markets drops too severely, or if for any other reason the United States doesn't look quite as safe a haven to foreigners as it has in the past, their attitude toward lending money could change. In fact, it did change in 1987 as far as private investors were concerned. So we are totally dependent on the central banks to meet the budget deficit of the United States government.

This is where I raise the question of independence, and it is really a question. I haven't come to any conclusions; my sole intention is to raise the issue. Are we exposing ourselves to economic limitations that will constrain future presidents' discretion in allocating domestic resources, and are we also limiting their ability to handle our foreign policy in ways that may be detrimental, if not dangerous, to the future of the United States? I cannot believe that a situation won't occur sometime in the next ten years in which the United States will find itself in disagreement with one of our major creditor nations. What happens then?

Take "Star Wars" as an example. "Star Wars" is as controversial abroad as it is at home. Suppose something occurred to make "Star Wars" even more controversial than it is today. One of our major creditors may say that if it continues to lend money to fund America's budget deficit it will, in effect, be funding "Star Wars." If a creditor opposes "Star Wars," it may make continued lending contingent upon our abandonment of "Star Wars." I don't suggest that this particular situation will occur, but it is the kind of predicament, it seems to me, that may very well occur. Since we are dealing not with thousands of private investors but with central banks, it doesn't take very many people to make a decision of that kind. This is the sort of concern that I am beginning to have, but I hope you can dispel it this afternoon and convince me to go home and forget about it.

There is a line of thought which says that it is better to be indebted to central banks than to private investors because private investors can panic or rush to get their money out—not only stop lending, as they did in 1987, but actually, God forbid, try to get their money back. Then you'd have a terrible time. The reasoning goes that central banks, being government agents, are stable and calm and take these things in stride. Thus, it's better to be dealing with the central bankers. There is some force to this argument. But underlying it all, whether they are private investors or central bankers, is the fact that we are exposing ourselves to decisions made by foreign nations which inevitably are made in their interest because that's the way nations make decisions. Those decisions made in their interest may not necessarily be in our interest and therefore may impinge in a very significant way upon the independence that Thomas Jefferson helped to bring about in 1776.

Perhaps that's enough at least to stimulate some violent disagreement, and I hope you can put my concern to rest.

**NARRATOR:** There is one other big question on which the senator has spoken before with the Miller Center Commission that Melvin Laird co-chaired, and that's the whole electoral process. We might leave a little time at the end for that. Why don't we turn first to the question of America's independence?

**QUESTION:** Senator, I wonder if our troubles aren't part of an even broader question, and that is whether or not our government structure has the ability to exercise the discipline that is necessary to achieve some reasonable balance. We have a situation now, it seems to me, in which there is an ever-widening demand for services of all kinds. However, there is a great reluctance to do what is necessary to pay for these services. The gap that exists between these two positions is now being filled by the central banks of the world. Is that a fair statement?

**SENATOR MATHIAS:** I think that is a fair statement. I particularly agree with you when you say that this is a very broad question. My hope is that sometime during this election year enough people will ask the candidates for

6

president questions on this subject, at least enough to force them to think about it. I have been a candidate often enough to know that candidates don't think all the time, and for a good reason. You get up at 5 or 6 a.m. and go off to a plant gate to shake hands, and then you go to a television station. Then you go to a fund-raising breakfast and so on until midnight when you drop into your bed and start all over again the next day. It is very easy to stop any kind of contemplative thinking. So I think it is up to the rest of us in the country to impress upon the candidates the necessity of thinking about this subject because I am convinced that the next president is not going to have a long period of repose after he moves into the White House before this subject is right on his doorstep. Whoever the next president may be, I think it is very necessary that he at least have some plan thought out well in advance as to what steps can be taken. The present administration has been very fortunate. It has an aura of confidence about it that keeps it afloat like the water beetle, but when you change presidents, it may be like the water beetle stopping to think—that's when our danger will come about.

QUESTION: Can we really count on such frankness on the part of the candidates, given the track record of experienced legislators who have met with resounding defeat when they advocated raising taxes as a means to increase revenue? I'm trying to think of the name of the man from Oregon who suggested, only in passing, the desirability of some form of broad-based tax in order to connect revenues with expenditures. And while he was an extremely able person, he was resoundingly defeated. I think Mr. Mondale would have something to say about how dangerous it is to suggest tax increases.

SENATOR MATHIAS: I am not under any illusion that we are going to get a ringing declaration to raise taxes out of any candidate in the field today. It is a very dangerous thing for a politician to do. Some of you may have known William Preston Lane who was governor of Maryland and a graduate of the University of Virginia, a very devoted alumnus of the University of Virginia. He, in a responsible way, advocated a sales tax for Maryland, and all he got in return was people throwing pennies at him as he left the governor's mansion. So this is a hard act, and I'm not unrealistic enough to expect a candidate to advocate a tax increase. But I want the candidates to think about it, and I want the platforms to begin to do something constructive in this field. If we don't, the ability of the president to preside as presidents have since 1789 is going to be curtailed.

**QUESTION:** A rather prominent Russian once said that democracy has within itself the seeds of its own destruction. We were organized not as a democracy but as a republic. Now we are operating as a democracy. Are we headed the way of Athens?

**SENATOR MATHIAS:** I'm not ready to throw in the towel yet, and leadership can make a tremendous difference here. This is another reason why it is important to raise these kinds of issues during a presidential election year.

I remember a conversation I had with Lyndon Johnson just a couple of days before he moved out of the White House. I had gone to pay a farewell call on the President, and he was in a rather philosophical mood. He asked me if I knew why he hadn't run for re-election. Then he began to tick off the reasons. One of them was the unrest and the difficulty of campaigning in the cities. He knew that would be very difficult. A second reason was that he wanted to get peace negotiations started, and he knew Ho Chi Minh would never start negotiations if he were a candidate. Ho Chi Minh would think it was all tinged with politics. He also said that the dollar needed a tax hike, and the Republicans wouldn't give it to him if he were a candidate. And for his fourth reason he pointed up to the picture of President Roosevelt, which was hanging over the fireplace, and said that he didn't want to leave the White House the way FDR did, in a box. But the point about wanting a tax increase to stabilize the dollar is, I think, an interesting one. The fact that he was willing to give up running for re-election because he wouldn't be able to get a tax increase to stabilize the economy is an admirable

8

attitude. Of course, you can make all sorts of judgments on what weight that one factor had in his decision not to run. Other things may have weighed more heavily, but nonetheless, that's a practical illustration of the kind of leadership I think it takes on the part of a president to get a tax bill through these days. You don't have to say you are going to raise taxes, but you can at least abstain from saying that you refuse under any conditions to consider additional revenues because, I think, a tax increase is in the cards.

QUESTION: Do you think we should change our election laws, particularly as far as contributions to congressional elections are concerned? Would that enable us to elect people who would stand up for fiscal responsibility?

SENATOR MATHIAS: I'm not sure that you can legislate the qualities of judgment and character that make for good legislators. You have to elect those people. I don't think you can have any formula by which you are going to limit membership in the Congress only to prudent, discreet, and careful people. That judgment is in the hands of the people. I am suspicious of formulas. Let me say to you that I have great reservations about a constitutional amendment for a balanced budget because I think there is no way you can substitute some phrase in the Constitution for the honest judgment of men and women serving in the Congress who know a job has to be done. If men and women serving in the Congress haven't made the commitment to do the job, they'll find a way to get around any words you might put in the Constitution.

In the state of Maryland we have a constitutional provision for a balanced budget, and we balance our budget every year. That, however, is the operating budget. We have a second set of books. We have a capital budget beyond the operating budget, and the capital budget represents a considerable amount of debt. So I don't think there are effective formulas, but I'd be interested in your thoughts on the matter.

**COMMENT:** Today, if a legislator takes a responsible position to raise taxes, not only will he be opposed by the man on the street; he may find himself challenged by an opponent with a good sum of political action committee (PAC) money. It seems to me that the PACs play a much larger role in electing our senators and congressmen than they used to. I'm wondering if this is one of the reasons that Congress doesn't seem to act as it did for 150 years to protect the people.

**SENATOR MATHIAS:** Well, that's a point we ought to pursue. But before we get too far away from the economic issue, let me just say that there is a kind of natural balance that I'm afraid will operate if we don't act soon. Every government since the time of Hammurabi that has become too deep in debt has found a way to get out of debt, and that is by debasing the coinage, by starting the printing presses. That's the way you gradually repudiate your debt. Of course this produces inflation. I think we can either come to a deliberate and careful decision on this, or we'll find that we have the natural solution imposed on us by the laws of economics. In the meantime we may also suffer from the fact that we've lost some control over our foreign policy.

But to address fairly your question about the electoral process, you are absolutely right: PAC money has become a major factor in elections in this country, and it has had a deleterious effect on the way the process works. Don't hold me too precisely to these figures, but in 1960 the percentage of eligible voters who voted in the presidential election was about 64 percent. In 1960, the cost of elections in the United States was $175 million. In 1984, twenty-four years later, voter participation had dropped to 53 percent, but the cost of elections had risen to $1.8 billion dollars. The cost had risen ten times. Yes, there was inflation in that twenty-four years. Prices rose by a factor of about two and a half. If you will apply that factor to those dollar figures, you will see that the cost of elections actually increased fourfold. It hasn't increased tenfold, but it has quadrupled in real terms. The 1984 elections cost about four times what the 1960 elections cost.

10

But here is the paradox. In 1984 we spent four times as much money as we did in 1960, yet we have 10 percent fewer people actually participating. You have only 53 percent compared to 64 percent. In the 1986 congressional elections—and, of course, congressional elections always have a slightly lower level of participation than presidential elections—the level of participation was only 36 percent, barely one third. So you have declining levels of participation and rising levels of cost. These become serious factors in how the government operates and how it is perceived.

I have a suggestion, but I'd like to hear yours as to what can be done to solve that problem?

**QUESTION:** Is there any way we could limit the length of the election period? It goes on and on and on, and this raises the cost.

**SENATOR MATHIAS:** Let me quote former Senator Howard Baker for a second time. He has some very ingenious suggestions that wouldn't even require an act of Congress. He proposes that the Federal Election Commission, which controls the matching funds that are handed out under the presidential election laws, should not recognize for matching purposes any expenditures that are made before January of the election year. So for this election, expenditures that occur in 1987 would not be matched with federal funds. This would mean that there wouldn't be that much campaign activity before 1988.

The second thing Baker proposes is that each party agree that it would seat delegates at their national convention only if they were elected in a particular month. It could be May; it could be June. It doesn't really matter in which they are elected, but that would compress the primaries and the election of delegates into a more limited period of time.

Thirdly, to give some continuity, to provide some institutional memory, he would mandate that incumbent governors and United States senators—the statewide officials—all be made automatic delegates to each party's convention. He thinks that with these three changes we

11

would substantially reduce the time period of the campaign and make it more efficient and effective.

My own solution would take it one step further. I would execute, now after a lapse of about eighty years, a recommendation that Theodore Roosevelt made in his State of the Union message of 1907 for public financing of congressional elections. I realize this wouldn't be very popular in many parts of the country. People cry that we can't afford it. Actually, it would be a money saver. Right now we are doing a considerable amount of campaign financing. We subsidize federal elections with the tax recognition we give to political contributions. That tax exemption has been costing the Treasury several hundred million dollars a year. We could finance the cost of congressional elections right now for considerably less than that. We can't limit the amount a candidate for Congress spends. The Supreme Court in the case of *Buckley vs. Valeo* (1976) ruled that campaign expenditures are a form of expression, and it would be a violation of the First Amendment to restrain that expression. I happen to think the Court was wrong. I think that the Congress has the right to control elections and could do so in that manner, but I'm not on the Court. Others are, and they have spoken. So we are limited really to the public financing method as a means of limiting expenditures and controlling the cost of elections, in addition to Howard Baker's three steps.

**NARRATOR:** Don't we already have governors and state officials at the conventions as super delegates?

**SENATOR MATHIAS:** Some are there, but not all. In the first place, public officials have to be elected as delegates. I don't mean to sound undemocratic, but I think statewide officials should be automatically seated. A public official can get into more trouble running as a delegate to the national convention than as a candidate for office. I ran to be a delegate at the 1984 Republican National Convention, and all of my critics seized that moment to rain down arrows upon my head. They accused me of being a liberal swine, to which I pleaded guilty, but it can be the kind of experience which is sufficiently unpleasant that it restrains people in office from undertaking it. Therefore, they simply let it pass and avoid that kind of an embarrassment which can create trouble for them in the next election. It is a problem if they have to run in an open primary. The super delegate arrangement is slightly different.

COMMENT: All of these suggestions presuppose that people become concerned about these things. I don't know how people are going to become concerned about these problems when they want to feel good, when they see millions of balloons coming out and the sun rising; they see people who are in important positions saying that things are all right, that we don't need to worry. There aren't many people around any more who remember the Great Depression and who realize that it can happen again. I think today there are a great many people who think this isn't going to happen, that it can't happen. So how are we going to make changes when everybody wants to feel good and when our leaders give us every reason to think that we should feel good?

SENATOR MATHIAS: That's exactly why I've come to Charlottesville, Virginia this afternoon. You are so right; when people want to feel good and when things are basically pretty positive, they are not going to insist on this kind of corrective action. Thoughtful people in the community have to assume leadership and the University of Virginia is the kind of place that needs to look at questions of this sort very carefully and to project ideas into the broader community. You may not arrive at solutions, but just raising awareness about the problems is a service. As long as I have a credit card in my pocket that somebody will honor, I can go on feeling good for a long, long time. But sooner or later the bill is going to be delivered at my door, and if I don't have the wherewithal to pay it, that's the end of my credit. It is that simple metaphor that we have to get across to people. We must get them thinking that the time has come to be serious about this. Not that we are going to go on the rocks in the next six months; I don't think that. I think, however, that within the next ten years we will face a real problem on the policy side as well as on the economic side. And it is only thoughtful people, those willing to look ahead, who can decide if this is a serious issue, and, if it is, to share their concern about what remedial action we can take.

**QUESTION:** Senator Mathias, considering all the economic problems the next president will face, how serious is the trade deficit and what would you do about it?

**SENATOR MATHIAS:** I would call it extremely serious because it is aggravating our foreign debt problem. That's one of the reasons we've moved from being the world's greatest creditor to the world's greatest debtor. And it is a much tougher problem than it appears. The annual trade deficit is currently in the area of $150 to $160 billion, but actually it is a bigger problem than that because you have to add on to the trade deficit the $50 billion in interest that you are going to pay to foreign creditors. Things may not get better soon. We should anticipate, that with the fall in domestic oil production, we are going to have to import more oil in the future than we have in the past. So in order to correct the trade deficit, the accounts deficit, we are going to have to look for a correction on the order of $200 billion, not a measly $150 billion. This is a problem of major magnitude.

I think that this will be on the new president's desk within a matter of weeks after he takes office because the foreign central bankers will want to send a message that they are not going to foot the American bill forever. Their own taxpayers will dictate that. There was a protest in the Netherlands in which the central bank of the Netherlands received complaints that the Dutch taxpayers should not be footing the bill for the American government's deficits.

Now you say, what should we do about the trade deficit? I think it takes a broad-based approach. We've learned that the easy solution which we thought would work, a lower dollar, is not going to solve the problem. It has helped. We are selling more of our goods overseas and this has reduced the trade deficit. But imports remain at a very high level, and you can hardly cut off imports to the

United States without seriously disrupting world trade. Any import restrictions would boomerang on us very quickly. So you simply have to work out arrangements, country by country, to improve the situation, and you have to improve the competitive structure of American industry. We have made a start on that. The Ford Motor Company has provided an outstanding example of improvement in the manufacturing process. We have opportunities and new technologies, such as fiberoptics, that offer hope for improving the trade situation. It is going to take this kind of broad-based, comprehensive approach. I don't believe that there is any single easy answer. There is no one law that Congress can pass or no one decree the president can sign that will solve it; what is required is a lot of leadership and a lot of discussion.

I remember when the Beatles were at their zenith that I was bemused by the fact that the Queen of England embraced them because they were one of the biggest earners of foreign capital in the British Isles. Funny as this may seem, it is the kind of thing I mean; the whole country must get behind the effort. The Beatles were bringing in trade pounds, and that was important to Britain and to the whole government, including the Queen, who went to work to applaud them and encourage them and tell other people to do likewise. I think that's the kind of measure of the task we face.

COMMENT: Reflecting on your comments with regard to independence, I find myself remembering that in our lifetime we have seen a gradual interdependence effort, through international organizations, not only in political but in health, humanitarian, and certainly economic areas. So much emphasis has been placed on the need for cooperation, that it is difficult to see how the independence emphasis, which I think many of us respect, can indeed be registered.

SENATOR MATHIAS: I acknowledge that there is a great deal of interdependence in the world today. The United States is interdependent with many nations. We look to Mexico, for example, for the largest amount of our imported oil. On the other hand, the Mexicans look to us for many

15

manufactured goods. So there is a considerable economic interdependence between Mexico and the United States. Neither one of us would do quite as well without the other. Indeed, I see interdependence as a desirable development in the international economy because I think it lends stability and depth to international relations.

But interdependence need not compromise national independence. The vision that concerns me has the United States five years down the road still without a balanced budget. Not having the domestic revenues to finance our deficit, we go to our usual bankers in Tokyo or Frankfurt or wherever, and they refuse to lend us any more money. In fact, they decide that they would like to have back some of the money they've already lent us. We say that this will cause a disruption in the United States, a depression, and all sorts of trouble. Realizing our predicament, they may use their influence to alter our foreign policy. That's what I call the loss of independence, which is different from being interdependent in a free and voluntary relationship. This is perhaps the worst and most drastic case.

An easier case to imagine is one in which we get into that kind of problem, and like many other countries in financial difficulty, we are forced to go to the International Monetary Fund. We know that the IMF imposes upon a debtor's domestic policy, often with harsh austerity measures. This is precisely what the IMF has done in the cases of Argentina and Brazil and with many other debtor nations. This is not a very far-fetched scenario.

**QUESTION:** You have suggested that the presidential candidates ought to have a good idea of how they are going to deal with our financial troubles. Certainly you are right, but isn't it possible that they could formulate a plan which they couldn't get through Congress?

**SENATOR MATHIAS:** One of the important things when entering the White House is to have at least some conception of what it is you want to do. I remember so well the time I went to a breakfast in the White House in the first week of the Nixon administration. In that first week President Nixon had made a few degrees shift in our relationship with the People's Republic of China. After breakfast, I told him that I had noticed what he had done and that I thought it was a constructive step. I wanted him to know that I supported him on it, and replied that this was only the beginning. Well, of course, it was just about four years later that Nixon was walking along the Great Wall of China. So he had arrived in the White House with that foreign policy concept. I would like to see the next president arrive in the White House with some conception of what to do about our economic problems, and it is important that he act early because it is very tough for a president to achieve all that he wants. And if there is any time for him to do so, it is during the first one hundred days of his presidency.

George Bush would not find this a new subject. You remember that he, after all, coined the phrase "voodoo economics," and what we are seeing today is one of the consequences of "voodoo economics." He had it exactly right when he said that. So I think with a little encouragement, George might begin to think about this subject.

Even if the candidates don't make their plans public because of the electoral risk, we can stimulate their internal thinking so that there is some motion on a vital subject that I think does jeopardize the work of Thomas Jefferson.

Thank you all for listening to me.

# II. The Presidency and the Constitutional System

### CONGRESSMAN RICHARD BOLLING

**NARRATOR:** Some years ago Congressman Bolling wrote in Volume V of *Papers of Presidential Transitions and Foreign Policy*:

> As I look back and think ahead to seek ways of improving the effectiveness of governmental systems, divided, complex, and always in transition, I am convinced that it is a mistake to examine any one political phenomenon as if it took place by itself. There must always be an attempt to at least set the stage, to look at the past and to examine the short and long range consequences of a particular political event. Politics is not a series of separate events; it is much more like a seamless web.

Congressman Bolling served as congressman from the Fifth District of Missouri during the tenure of eight presidents, from the Eighty-first to the Ninety-sixth Congress. He occupied a number of crucial positions as chairman of the Select Committee on Committees of the House of Representatives; chairman of the Rules Committee; chairman of the Joint Economic Committee; a member of the Steering and Policy Committee of the Democratic Caucus and of the House Budget Committee.

Lest you think that his background is exclusively that of the politician, he was Chub Fellow at Yale University and Fellow at the Center for Advanced Studies at Wesleyan

University and taught and lectured in Kansas City. He was a Lieutenant Colonel in the United States Army and received the Distinguished Congressional Service Award from the American Political Science Association. He probably is the only person who will visit the Center who was ever elected to the *Sports Illustrated* Twenty-fifth Anniversary All-American Football Team. He is the author of *House Out of Order* and *Power in the House*, which first appeared in 1968 and is now in a revised edition.

**CONGRESSMAN BOLLING:** I'd like to talk a little bit about the last five presidents. I don't want to offend anybody, most particularly at the beginning, but I think that four of the last five presidents have been failures. They've been failures in utterly different ways. The one I do not consider a failure professionally is Jerry Ford, but that may be my prejudice because he and I were friends and still are, despite the fact that we disagree on virtually every domestic item one can think of. Still, we disagree in a way that is less than disagreeable. We disagree because we believe differently and we understand the political process. I had the opportunity to be very close to a few of the last five presidents, not very close to all of them, but I had the opportunity to observe all of them.

I didn't retire from Congress until after President Reagan's first two years as President, but he wasn't the reason I retired. Circumstances kept me from feeling that I had to stay. I retired relatively young for a congressman, but with no difficulties or political opposition. I retired because I thought it was time to do something else. Basically, it was to try and help all of the people in academia who have devoted their lives to studying how government works.

I thought that my responsibility as a congressman was to lead and to educate, and I thought education was the right role all the time. I still feel that way, but I found it much more difficult to do what I had planned when I retired. The simple reason was that I still could learn. So I read a lot, particularly about the Constitution and constitutional history, and found it very difficult to come to a final conclusion. Fairly recently, I attempted a book and wrote a chunk of it and decided I didn't like it. I'm now on my fourth redraft, and you are going to get the benefit, or bear the burden, of hearing my conclusions.

I supported a candidate who is now out of the Democratic race for the presidency. I supported him to avoid what I believe were the reasons why four of our last five presidents failed. I shall tell you what I have as positive recommendations for any president in the future.

Lyndon Johnson failed because he wasn't balanced. He tried to do too much. I happen to agree with what he tried to do in almost all the domestic cases. I think we were way behind on the things that needed to be done with the poor and the weak in society, but I think he overreached himself, and I think nothing could be done to stop him.

His successor, to my utter amazement, may turn up in history as professionally a pretty good president. Nixon was a crook and I always thought he was a crook; I despised Richard Nixon. To say that he might turn out to be a pretty good president in retrospect is a shock to me. Nixon did great damage to the republic. The fact that a president could be forced to retire hurt the political process severely.

Carter came to Congress with many pleasant and some very good ideas. He was very bright and very able, but wholly incompetent to be president because he couldn't deal with Congress at all, ever. From the beginning he failed with Congress and alienated his congressional allies, virtually from his first days in office. I think he would have been a good president, by the way, in the second term because he learned a lot, but he was a terrible president in the first term. Aside from Congress, he turned off the American people and that didn't help.

Now I'm going to say very little about Ronald Reagan, but I'll say something rather definitive, and I'm going to say it right now: I think he is the worst president that ever served the United States of America.

There is one characteristic of all four presidents that I consider failed, and in some cases it goes against the myths of our time. For example, Lyndon Johnson was unable to creatively work with the Congress. The great myth is that Lyndon Johnson was a genius with the Congress; the fact is that he never was even a successful legislator. He was a successful politician in the House; when he was in the Senate and became Senate leader, he was a great manipulator of senators. He did not deal very well with any constituency except his own Texas constituency. He did that rather well, though in ways that I did not always admire. But that is beside the point.

When he became President, he failed to pay attention to anybody when he created his programs, unless they were going in the direction that he wanted to go. And everything he wanted to do, he wanted to do in the first year of his elected presidency. He succeeded Jack Kennedy in 1963 and served through 1964 and the election, but only after he was elected President did he become overwhelmed by himself.

By that time, his friends who had had the power to check him in the past were either dead or gone. Sam Rayburn died in 1961 and he was the only person who could really sit Lyndon Johnson down. His great friend in the Senate, Richard Russell of Georgia, was no longer there to influence him effectively, and he listened to no one. His imbalance made him a failure, not just in Vietnam but also in domestic policy and, in particular, in economic policies. He couldn't and didn't work with the House, he just ran over it, and he tried to run over the Senate. He didn't learn from the institution.

Obviously, the same thing is true of Nixon. Nixon did a better job of working with the House, but he didn't work honestly with it. If you remember those days and if you watched events carefully, it was rather fascinating to see what happened. At first, the Committee on the Judiciary that dealt with the Watergate investigation was composed mostly of liberal Democrats who were concerned about Richard Nixon and what he had done. Then most of the moderate Democrats joined up, followed by the conservative Democrats. Eventually the most liberal Republicans were also swayed until virtually all Republicans were there as well. Even then some were still saying, that although they didn't really like him, they believed him. Still, there was a shift. The only time he really worked with Congress was the time when it was really working against him. He was never completely honest with the Congress; he never took advantage of all the people that could have helped him in Congress.

Carter was hopeless. I'm going to talk about this from the positive side. Carter had a legislative liaison team that honestly believed that the Congress of the United States was a little bit lower than the legislature of the State of Georgia. I grew up in northern Alabama, so I'm not anti-Georgia or anti-South. The liaison team simply didn't have any comprehension of what the House of Representatives was like; they did not even understand the constitutional sense of what the House of Representatives was supposed to be. They treated everybody as if they were slaves—people were supposed to automatically do what the President wanted. It was a disaster.

Mr. Reagan, on the other hand, was enormously successful with the Congress in the first year. You won't believe it because you don't see it in the press, but after that first year, he hardly ever won another fight. A few times he won on issues related to the Iran-Contra affair, but on economic issues, like taxes in 1982, the Republicans in the Senate turned against him. We passed a tax bill that did exactly the opposite of what Ronald Reagan wanted until he accepted it. He swore for months that he would never sign a tax bill that increased taxes, yet taxes were substantially increased in 1982, primarily due to the efforts of Senator Robert Dole. That is certainly interesting considering the way things are today.

For reasons of politeness, I'm not going into the rest of Reagan's eight years. I'm not sure that what I have to say would be completely balanced. I may not give him enough credit for cheering up the country. He did that. I may not give him enough credit for some of the things that have happened in foreign policy. Usually, it seems to me, good things happened *despite* him, but they have happened and they are very important.

So we have had, in my view, a disastrous breakdown in our system of separated powers starting after the death of Jack Kennedy. And in a system like ours, unless all the players understand that they must share power, we do not get a government capable of governing the country. The only time a similar breakdown occurred was during the Civil War, and obviously there was no government that suited all the people of the country at that time. That's the only time the political process has completely broken down.

23

The political process of this country is, in my judgment, the most difficult political process in the world. At least one can reasonably and honestly say, that we have popular government, free government, and democratic government with republican procedures.

We have a country so complicated that even when there were only thirteen states, you wonder how it came to be. You wonder how those people were able to put together the Constitution, and more importantly, how the document was ratified. The wonderful thing about the Constitution is that is was ratified. There have been many constitutions written in                )ur Constitution was ratified and
                                        n at peace with ourselves and to
(                                       was largely the result of the
c                                       the president, and the Supreme
C                                       nship with each other on almost
e                                       am saying, in effect, that you
ca                                      )vernment, no matter how bright
a                                       informed he is about the issues,
ur                                      work with the Congress.

                 may think that is fine as long as the Congress and the president are of the same party. We read a great deal about how our government has broken down because different parties control different bodies. Yet the greatest accomplishments of this country's federal government have been achieved with bipartisan support. Our victory in World War II was such an accomplishment. I guess there are a good many people who know that that war wasn't a cinch, that an Allied victory was not certain. There were, after all, two wars being fought, one in the Pacific and the other in Europe, and in each case there was a very good possibility that we were going to lose. Winning both wars was a bipartisan accomplishment, done with Presidents Roosevelt and Truman working closely with the Congress.

It is remarkable that even when Truman faced a Republican House, most of the important things he wanted to do in foreign policy and defense were done. The Eightieth Congress, which he used as a political whipping boy on domestic policy in 1948, was the Congress through which much of the great program went. On foreign affairs there was a residue of cooperative attitudes and an understanding that we had to work together. I am

24

reasonably sure that at least in modern times, unless presidents are really able to work closely with members of the opposite party, they can't implement programs which will last. I think Johnson pushed his programs so strongly that there was a backlash which undid many of those needed programs. This could have b̲̲᷉᷉᷉᷉ ̲ded if he had been more moderate.

The key is tl                              stand how to work with the Cong                              House. Why is the House so in                              so important because it is the onl                              ich all of the concerns of the Am                              nable chance to penetrate. The                              nt the great issues; the House                              people in congressional district          ...... lobbyists. The people who don't have lots of money or numerical support have an opportunity to talk to members of the House. That makes the House more difficult to deal with than the Senate, especially because there are 435 members rather than 100. Its complexity, though, is one of the reasons the House is so fascinating. When you pass major legislation in the House, you are consciously putting all the great interest groups of the country together, first in a contest and then in a cooperative effort. If presidents don't understand that, and don't work with the House on that kind of a basis, they cannot possibly work successfully with the government as a whole.

I could talk about the Supreme Court or the bureaucracy, and I am prepared to talk about a variety of other things if you ask me questions. There is one key point I want to make, and though I may just sound like an old, retired member of the House recalling how important his work was, that really isn't the point. I believe firmly that this country has forgotten the role of the House. By and large, it is true not just for presidents but for the whole country. The academic community has forgotten it because most academics don't like to spend the time that's necessary to understand the House of Representatives and how it works.

I'll tell you an anecdote and then I'll stop. Years and years ago, the most distinguished of all the journalists of his time, Walter Lippmann, invited me to lunch. He invited me to a club that I wouldn't belong to for reasons that you may have detected in what I've said and what I will say. It amused me. It was a nice club and it was perfectly proper for him to be there, but it was not a group in which I was going to be involved for several reasons. We had a lovely, wonderful luncheon which lasted four hours. I couldn't believe it. The last hour or so I was trying to get away because I just didn't believe that I should be taking up a great man's time. I didn't agree with Walter Lippmann on an awful lot of things, but I admired him. My press friends thought that he was a second coming of sorts. I don't mean to be disrespectful in saying that, but they really revered him. I didn't really know why he had asked me to lunch, but we spent a long time talking about nothing but the House. He asked the questions and I answered quickly and briefly.

For a long time I didn't hear anything from him and I simply did my job in the House. Finally I heard, as I knew I'd hear in time, why he wasn't picking up on anything we had spoken about, and why I didn't hear from him again. Lippmann is supposed to have said, "You know, the young man was really very interesting. He said all kinds of things that I knew to be accurate and was giving me a really wonderful description of the institution. But I've decided it was just too complicated for me to get involved in, and I am not going to do anything more about it."

I will submit to you that that's what all the media people have decided, with the exception of a few, and too many others have decided the same. Further, I would submit to you that if that isn't understood by either the people or the presidents, our system is going to break down. It isn't going to work unless we have presidents who understand that they have to work with the House and how to work with the House.

Jack Kennedy died having had the greatest congressional relations team there ever was. The Republicans in the Eisenhower administration and in this administration have had consistently good congressional relations. We shall need better congressional relations with the president if we are going to make the policy decisions we must make.

**QUESTION:** I recently read a book that claimed that Richard Nixon was brilliant in dealing with foreign policy and cited his recognition of China and agreements with Russia as examples. Would you agree with that assessment?

**CONGRESSMAN BOLLING:** Yes. I know less about the details of the Brezhnev agreements, but I do think that the opening with China was crucial and long overdue. I thought it was ridiculous that this issue frightened a lot of politicians. It didn't have to, but it did. However, the people weren't very frightened by the idea. A demagogue like McCarthy or Nixon, in his own day, could rouse up and frighten some people. But just plain, ordinary, moderate people weren't shocked if you said you were in favor of opening relations with China. I always put it on a simple *quid pro quo* basis: We would certainly recognize China if they'd give us something in return. It didn't have to be anything tangible, simply an assurance, for example, that they would be friendlier, or let's say, less unfriendly.

**QUESTION:** Congressman Bolling, you have indicated how important it is for an incoming president to be able to work with the Congress. Is there anything on the other side, something that Congress needs to do? What do you see, particularly in the transition between the election and the inauguration that might be accomplished?

**CONGRESSMAN BOLLING:** I think Congress needs to do a number of things to improve the transition. I think there should be more money made available for a newly-elected president, whether it is George Bush or some Democrat. There should be the opportunity to do some things very quickly, and it takes money to do that. The Congress already has a burden, in my opinion, to improve the formal transition—the approach to the transition. The Congress has to have a sense of responsibility to the president.

I don't think I exaggerate in saying this: The *president* more or less determines how partisan the Congress is with his own behavior. I'm talking about Congress as an entity, as an institution. If the president is friendly and sticks to his word, and tries to be cooperative with both individuals and institutions, he'll ultimately get a pretty good reaction.

If he is confrontational and determined to make political hay out of situations, it can get pretty ugly. But the president also has the power to cool down those situations.

It got pretty ugly in the 1940s, in Truman's time. But Truman never lost the people with whom he had to work effectively in foreign policy and defense to get results. He would blast the Republicans on domestic policy and fume about the no-good Eightieth Congress, yet he maintained his relationships with Vandenberg and people in the House who were equally important. In order to get things through the House, he had to have the support of some Republicans.

I think the president has the initiative because he is, after all, the most powerful politician there is, and the most powerful legislator. Everybody forgets that the president is a legislator, though it is odd that they do. He is a legislator because he has a veto, and all he has to do is veto something and he raises the ante almost out of sight. Getting two-thirds of the votes in the House, or in the Senate, is very different than getting the majority. That veto is a tremendous source of influence. I'm not trying to put all the burden on the president. I would be shocked if a Democratic speaker did not respond to a legitimate, nonpartisan request from the president.

I don't know how it looks from the outside. The media deal with things as they wish (though I don't mean to be a media-basher). I worked with them very closely for many years, and the media just did not give Congress much of a chance to be understood simply because they didn't have enough people covering it. There are probably only a half dozen papers in the United States that have real coverage of the House. The media cover what is relatively easy to cover. You can cover the president very easily. Sam Donaldson could cover the president by himself, and he will be able to supply the whole network with news about the president reasonably well. It isn't hard to keep up with the Supreme Court either; that also can be dealt with by one person. Similarly, one person can deal remarkably well with one hundred senators, partly because the Senate is run entirely differently. But when you get to the House, you are dealing with complexity. I don't know how to solve that problem, but I think that's *the* problem.

I cannot conceive of a House Speaker in this era who would be an affront to the president. It has happened to other presidents, Lincoln, for example, who was accosted by the radical element of his own party. Roosevelt too, had an incident or two when his leadership in the Senate resigned on him because he bad-mouthed a senator for what he had said about the wartime tax bill. Roosevelt was dead right, by the way; it was a lousy tax bill, but he shouldn't have made it known the way he did. In any event, that's all they could get and they had worked very hard on it. Alben Barkley resigned in a huff, and Roosevelt had to beg him to come back. I recognize the problem. If Robert Michel [House Minority leader] turned out to be the Speaker and a Democrat were elected, he'd be just as worried about being good to the president as I would, or anybody else who was on the Democratic side.

COMMENT: To carry on the same line of thought, the House seemed to be easier to understand in the days of a very strong Speaker and a half dozen strong committee chairmen with whom the president might have rapport and considerable contact. The reorganization of the House seems to present, at least to the public view, the presence of a considerable array of power centers. Therefore, the institution is harder to understand and deal with. Looking at it from the inside, how is the House mobilized into effective majorities?

CONGRESSMAN BOLLING: That's hard to answer because you have to recognize a number of myths first. Some of you may know that I worked very closely with Sam Rayburn for the last ten years of his life. Sam Rayburn had very little power compared to the institutional power of Carl Albert, Tip O'Neill, or the current Speaker. Most of the time he was defeated by the committees. Sam Rayburn could only do what was possible, given the committee system. For the most part, the committee system of Congress was controlled by a coalition of conservative southern Democrats and almost all Republicans from 1938 until 1961. The Democrats from the South were conservative, the Republicans from the Middle West were conservative, and of course conservatives came from other places too.

The truth of the matter is that Roosevelt completely lost control of Congress from about 1939 on. Sam Rayburn was sort of his emissary who tried to do something with Congress. Rayburn had great power to change a few votes. He had gathered up his chips in the classic way. His power lasted the longest, I think, in the history of the House. He had been a committee chairman in 1931 and then Speaker until he died in 1961. I don't know of any other political career that was like that. I happen to believe that Rayburn was the greatest legislator of all time. But he didn't have all that power usually attributed to him.

The *institutional* power of the present Speaker is substantially greater. Rayburn looked powerful because on the surface he stayed out of the committee problems. He controlled two committees and dominated one. He controlled the majority of the Ways and Means Committee on a crucial item—taxes—in a way that I didn't agree with, especially taxes on oil and gas. He also controlled it in a way I did agree with in regard to trade, but he didn't really control it beyond that. He didn't control the Rules Committee for most of his career. Howard Smith of Virginia was more powerful than Sam Rayburn in the House of Representatives regarding the flow of legislation, and so were some other committee chairmen. Sam Rayburn was for a Tennessee Valley Authority in another part of the country, in the Northwest. It was blocked by a committee chairman who was powerful enough to defy Rayburn and, as a matter of fact, defy his committee and defy the House. So there are all kinds of myths that one needs to get rid of.

Nevertheless, Rayburn was a great legislator. If the Eisenhower people came to him, or if Eisenhower himself had him down for a drink and a chat, Rayburn would tell them the truth. I've listened to Rayburn on the telephone, saying, "But Ike, you can't do that." So Rayburn was up there telling them what they could and couldn't do, and they'd work things out so that they wouldn't try to do the impossible, unless they wanted to do it for political purposes. You had an entirely different view of what was really going on; Rayburn was getting whipped over and over again. I could tell you some hair-raising anecdotes about how little power he had.

You are, however, absolutely right that the legislative process has been seriously impaired by the increase in subcommittees, and probably by the increase in subcommittee staffs. I'm not sure about the impact of the staff increase, but I am sure that the subcommittees have damaged the legislative process. And the reason I'm sure of it is because the only way you could deal with it was through the Rules Committee. You had to be able to have a debate on the floor that was coherent, and the only way you could take four, five or six different committees and make their product coherent, sensible, and fair was by a rule of debate that was very intricate and complicated. If we hadn't been able to do that, the House would have collapsed in a general chaos, and it still could. It very badly needs to be reorganized in terms of committee jurisdictions.

As you probably know, I chaired a committee at the time when we adopted the Budget Act that failed. We got a lot of other interesting things done but not the crucial thing, which was to reorganize the committee system. I am all for modification of the committee system regarding seniority, and I'm all against the subcommittees. I think we need a president to help us on that, by the way, but he [President Reagan] never says out loud that he is for anything.

QUESTION: Would you care to comment on immigration policies? There seems to be a lack of consensus on the issue.

CONGRESSMAN BOLLING: I have a hard time with the premise that immigrants hurt us because I'm old enough to remember the Irish immigrants and the refugees from middle Europe in the 1940s. I think Hispanic immigrants are doing something *for* us as well as *to* us. They are obviously competitive, and they have different religious and cultural attitudes. In the 1940s, Irish-Americans dominated Kansas City politics for years and years. It had happened earlier in the Northeast, in the Boston area, and so on.

I may be foolish, but I think that this country can absorb this diversity. Perhaps the most remarkable thing

31

that we have given the world is our extraordinary ability to absorb diversity.  While I don't think it is quite as remarkable as the Constitution and its development, I think the political system is very remarkable.  Our ability to absorb variety in a semi-civilized way is very important.  I don't think we should turn down people who disagree with us religiously, or in other ways.

**QUESTION:**  But does it fractionalize the country?

**CONGRESSMAN BOLLING:**  I think that is one of the fractionalizations you have to face; that fractionalization is represented in the House.  There now is a vast constituency of people who come from another country, and most of the people they elect remain diverse.  But the diversity is not creating a whole lot of political divisions, though it is doing so to some degree.

Let me tell you about my successor.  He is a black man representing a constituency that is 75 percent white. When I decided to retire, which I did very early, a year before I had to file for the primary, a young black legislator, who had come from a black district, decided he would run for Congress.  He did so despite the fact that the district was three-quarters white, and if I may say so inelegantly, there are quite a few "rednecks" in that district.

A lot of people didn't think he had a chance to get nominated.  I stayed out of the nominating process because I knew that I wouldn't have anything useful to do if I got myself involved in it early.  He got himself nominated and won, although the odds were against him.  The skeptics said, "Kansas City is not going to elect him.  The people are not ready to elect a black."  In any event Alan Wheat got elected and reelected a couple of times, and he is probably going to have a great, not just good, congressional career.

I think this proves something unique.  There is maybe one other district in the country—I'm not absolutely sure about it—where a black man represents a majority white constituency.  It may be true in the Berkeley, California district where Ron Dellums runs, though Ron Dellums and Alan Wheat are very different people.  It seems to me that we have something very interesting happening. The people of Kansas City are plain, ordinary American people, largely white, and very heterogeneous in terms of where they came from. But they have voted for Wheat repeatedly. I don't know how meaningful this is, except that it makes me feel pretty optimistic about the American people and their ability to think about their problems.

When they think about the problems that they have, they may seem very acute. They need to think about the problems America has in the world and its responsibility in the world. It wouldn't do us a bit of harm if we had a better understanding about the religions and cultures of the Far East, the Middle East, and Africa. I myself am guilty of not knowing the African religions and the attitudes associated with them. Suppose we had more people from these backgrounds living in this country? We would learn very quickly what the problems are in the countries they come from, as if we lived with them.

I had an experience today that I thought was absolutely fascinating. We wanted to have a sandwich before we came here. We pulled up at a place which called itself a deli. It was out in the country, and it was a very nice place. It turned out that the proprietor was a man from Iran. He had been a film maker and fled Iran because he had been involved in making a film for the government of the Shah. But the proprietor was defending Iran as being attacked unfairly by Iraq, despite the fact that he had been run out of the country. He would surely have been killed if he'd stayed, but here he was still defending his country, though not his government. I don't think that's a bad thing, to have such a diner sitting on a highway in Virginia.

QUESTION: I am thinking about your Lippmann anecdote and the fact that nobody wants to hear about the House. I wonder if you can allay my fears about the negative attitudes toward Congress and specifically the House which have developed in our culture.

There was a moment last summer during the Iran-Contra hearings when I thought that Brendon Sullivan [Oliver North's lawyer] was saying, in coaching Oliver North, "The way we can win this thing is to make it a battle of North against Congress; a solitary military hero and patriotic figure against congressional characters, many of whom are old crocodiles." That played pretty well. To me it showed that the understanding of what this institution is all about wasn't there. Let me formulate it this way: the attitude contained more than boredom or disinterest; it contained a certain animus against Congress. This President can say, "All North did was not tell Congress everything; I do that myself," and get a laugh. There is a lot of negative imagery surrounding Congress, and specifically the House. I feel that it has increased, and there was a moment last summer when the negative image of Congress became very strong. I hope you can tell me that I'm wrong.

**CONGRESSMAN BOLLING:** No, I don't think you are wrong. Part of the reason is that Congress needs very badly to reorganize itself, the House in particular. I am not sure about the Senate because I simply don't understand the Senate as well as I do the House. But the House desperately needs to have a reorganization that makes it work somewhat better. I think reorganization is possible with the help of a very well organized set of lobby groups on the outside to assist in convincing individual members of the House of the need to reorganize and with a president who is not hostile.

Some legislation with which I was involved and which would have reorganized the institution very substantially was not a cinch to lose. It didn't get passed because we made a few mistakes, because of bad luck, and, unlike the issue on which the Budget Act rode into being, because it didn't get good press. We had reasonably good support from a variety of places, but we didn't get good press. While I think it is absolutely essential that the Congress do that, I don't think it will happen without a president who is understanding of Congress.

One of the bad breaks that we had on that Select Committee of Committees was that Ford, who helped set up the committee, left the House. Carl Albert consulted with Ford, when he was still in the House, on setting up the Select Committee on Committees. It would have helped us if Ford had been there, and it would have helped institutional reform if he had remained in the presidency because he was friendly. We need a president who understands the House and who is clever enough to be able to convey his sympathy, though he can't afford to go public with it. If he goes public with his support, he automatically creates opposition among representatives who fear that the president is trying to interfere in their districts. That simply isn't so. Jack Kennedy was in on the fight we had in 1961, which gave the power to control the flow of legislation back to the Speaker as opposed to Howard Smith, but he never acknowledged this publicly.

Maybe there's another thing that we ought to talk about on this. A lot of what happens in Congress has to be secret in the preliminary stages. There is no way on earth that you can work out a very difficult political issue unless you do it in secrecy. That does not mean that your acts in a committee or on the floor should not be recorded. Everybody's votes should be known. But when you begin to work on a very difficult problem like the Marshall Plan or the first Civil Rights Act, you have to have secrecy because the people, who represent districts and interest groups, have to have a chance to go back with a plan to consult with at least some of their constituents on what will work. When you get into the process, you have to go completely public. So you need secrecy in the conceptual stage. The best example of that is of course the Constitution. They had to have secrecy initially, or they never could have gotten this document passed that won state by state by very narrow margins. When you are fighting with narrow margins politically, you simply must have the ability to put together your piece without public knowledge. All bipartisan efforts are done that way. Part of the problem, then, is that Congress can't defend itself.

QUESTION: I have two questions. One is rather general and the other is more precise. The first one has to do with your view that President Johnson was a failure. I am interested in how you would contrast him with Kennedy. And more specifically, my recollection is that Johnson secured the passage of legislation that Kennedy couldn't get through Congress. Is that correct?

CONGRESSMAN BOLLING: That's right.

35

**QUESTION:** As I understand your view, it is that despite Johnson's civil rights legislation and his war on poverty, he was a failure because he disturbed relations with Congress and because some of his legislation went too far.

**CONGRESSMAN BOLLING:** No, each of these presidents was different. Johnson passed all kinds of legislation that Kennedy couldn't get through. You don't have to look very far to see why. Kennedy never had anything like a friendly Congress. Johnson passed very important civil rights laws. I happen to know a great deal about them as I was involved in the details, including when Johnson shifted the priorities from the tax cut first—which was Kennedy's approach—to civil rights. Johnson used the sympathy for Kennedy to do something dramatic about civil rights. It was magnificent. I think Johnson was a great president, as well as a failed president, because of that.

Incidentally, the civil rights legislation had already passed the House under Kennedy. Johnson, however, reversed the Senate by using the power of the presidency. That deserves a lot of credit. On the other hand, he not only ran over Congress, but also ignored advice from Congress. He'd always taken it when it had come from Rayburn's mouth. Later, there was nobody there that he'd listen to, not a soul. He made excessive demands because he never argued the case for how much should be done later on.

In 1965 when all the great programs that should have come up in 1945 came up in smaller measure, he received an overwhelming majority, which he then misused. We never did achieve anything substantial about the District of Columbia because he overreached himself. He didn't maintain a balanced approach, although some of the things he did were wonderful. Nevertheless, he didn't handle the economy well; he caused the inflation to start. Also, of course, I don't think he dealt very well with the Vietnam situation. But I don't want to make an issue out of that; I just think he overdid it. He pressured congressmen rather than worked with them.

I am trying to say that Congress produces some wisdom as well as some clowns.

**QUESTION:** It looks like the budget touches right on that subject. Could you give some examples of legislation that, in your opinion, he went too far on? My second question concerns your view of the recent proposal that the president be given a line item veto.

**CONGRESSMAN BOLLING:** Well, I'm one of the very few Democrats who is basically for the line item veto, and this is why: I think it will take away some of the power committee chairmen shouldn't have, such as getting a number of pet projects passed when they aren't really justified.

I served as chairman of the Rules Committee for a number of years, and I had too much power. Nobody should have that much power. In the last six months of a two year term I had more power over legislation than the president. I realize that's an awfully strong statement, but I had life or death power on virtually any piece of legislation unless it had unanimous support. That power of congressmen needs to be curbed. I shall even name such a congressman. Jamie L. Whitten has taken such good care of Mississippi that it is amazing to me that there is anything wrong in Mississippi. I don't think people should be allowed to do what Jamie L. Whitten did, and I think only a line item veto can do it.

This raises a lot of problems, of course, and if it goes through, it will go through on a great, big, complicated deal where power is shared in different ways. Perhaps it will go through on a complicated lousy deal, which is related to the legislative veto. I don't know, but that's how things get done in the real world. It may turn up, for all I know, in the modifications of the Budget Act which very badly needs to be modified. I'm not giving you a very optimistic answer. It is going to be a tough piece of work.

Regarding the examples of excessive demands made by Johnson, I think the example of the Office of Economic Opportunity (OEO) is the saddest one, and at the same time the most important bill among those that should have been done moderately. The OEO should have been started out relatively small with a good many of the principles included, but he kept it growing like Social Security. He wanted to get constituency for it and keep it there. I don't pretend to be able to list all these bills without going back and looking them up. Generally speaking, the ones that Nixon knocked out are the ones that went too far, and the ones that survived Nixon's attempts at elimination are the ones that were done right. That's a very pragmatic explanation, but it is fairly accurate. If Nixon couldn't get rid of them, then they were probably pretty well accepted.

In other words, legislation shouldn't be acceptable only in a partisan sense, but it should be sustainable in a broadly-gauged national sense if it is to last. The legislature and the president, in my view, have a responsibility for not putting too much on the table. Johnson's program, if looked at in economic terms was nuts, although I loved all the ideas it contained.

QUESTION: Is a bipartisan foreign policy possible? If so, would you please address U.S. policy toward the Soviet Union in this context?

CONGRESSMAN BOLLING: Yes, we can have a bipartisan foreign policy. This is one of the areas, however, in which I can't be polite about President Reagan. My main criticism of President Reagan is that he doesn't do his job; his job is not to be a cheerleader, but to be the master of our foreign and defense policy and to maintain a society that is stable. For a society to be stable it has to be relatively at peace with itself, which makes necessary all the social legislation I have talked about.

I don't think President Reagan has ever known enough about the realities of foreign policy to be a president. I don't think he has ever tried to know enough. I have been scared to death of his lack of knowledge about the defense establishment. I'm not against the defense establishment as such; I think it is crucial that we have a strong defense. While I have been against some weapons systems, I have supported others. Generally I'm thought of as a hawk, at least by my critics. But I don't think we need to have the kind of military base we have been building. We've been throwing money at the military in a way Johnson threw money at domestic programs. I think that is madness and that we have a real problem.

For years we tried to put together a bipartisan consensus in Congress to reform the defense establishment. It began after I retired in 1981-82. I was fascinated to watch it. Perhaps it was a reaction to what I consider Reagan's excess, compared to the reasonable increase in defense undertaken by Carter. (I mean the first time Carter increased defense spending, not the second time when he seemed to sweeten the pot and perhaps was playing politics as he left the presidency.)

In any event, Senator Sam Nunn and a variety of other people, not all of whom I know very well, are very busy trying to rationalize our defense establishment and defense policy. Behind that, of course, is the need for a rational foreign policy and behind that is the competition with the Soviet Union. My view on the Soviet Union hasn't changed an iota. I have been almost a professional anti-Stalinist, although Stalin has been dead for a long time.

Despite that, I feel that at all times you have to be in communication with the Soviet Union as much as with China. Presently I'm a little bit less of a hard-liner than I was. But I'll probably be more of a hard-liner in the next years for the reason that the American people will be in one of their euphoric phases when they think of the Soviet Union as a friend. I won't be. I think we have to have a balanced defense; I think we have to be careful about our commitments; I think we have a major responsibility in the democratic world. Part of that requires an aggressive effort to get along with the Soviet Union and reduce the piles of weapons for which we really don't have much use. We ought to keep the ones we need.

QUESTION: I wonder what would happen if we had an ideological and stubborn president who could use the line item veto and deny the House the right to override? Wouldn't he be able to destroy months or years of legislation?

CONGRESSMAN BOLLING: That's a very good question. Superficially the answer probably would be that he could. But the fact of the matter is that when you get into these struggles the people who turn out to be ideological fanatics are relatively few in number. Nevertheless, today we are facing for the first time in my experience a significant number of people who have decided that near-fanaticism is the only way in which the Republicans will regain the House. So you have some very bright people, including a man from Georgia named Newt Gingrich, who are very far to the right and insist on being confrontational.

I don't think they are going to succeed. I think so because I've met enough Republicans in meetings where we were not conferring as partisans but as people who wanted to get things done. The last thing we need today is the confrontational approach taken by a few Republican fanatics. What we need, with our economic difficulties, which in my opinion are enormous, is civility. Even though we still have a remnant of euphoria about the economy, at least in some parts of the population, I see problems ahead. I hate to use the word that some people think indicates weakness, but "civility" is one of the things that we very badly need in the times ahead.

Let me just engage in a short discourse on the problem of civility. At this moment we are in the election process. That's the time to fight. If possible, you ought to do it in a way that is educational, but now is the time to do it. When everybody is elected and has become part of the government, that's the time to work together. It isn't very smart to play party electoral politics year-round. You ought to be able to confine your party politics to election time, and regardless of whether you win or lose, be civil about the outcome.

Take those people who supported the Constitution. Those people had been at each other's throats on previous occasions. Jefferson and Hamilton, for example, had violently differing views. But they knew they had to work together once the controversy about the Constitution was settled. In the same way we have somehow to get the American people and the Congress to work together, and the president has to learn that first. Then we won't have to worry about the item veto and legislative conflict.

If Harry Truman could get Vandenberg and company, who comprised very large numbers in the House and Senate, to consent to a bipartisan foreign policy, why can't anybody else?

**NARRATOR:** One of the legitimate criticisms of social science and academic work is that so often it is too far removed from the patient in the bed, and doesn't deal with the real issues. Dick Bolling's service in the Eighty-first to the Ninety-sixth Congress amounted to some thirty-four years in which he was very close to the patient in the bed, and he is quite willing to diagnose the condition of the patient. That's why it is so important to have him here today to speak about a very neglected problem in American political history and political practice. We are all extremely grateful to him for coming.

# III. The President and Congress

## JEFFREY BERGNER

**NARRATOR:** Last August I read what I thought was a very challenging and provocative piece, called *The Political Realignment of American Foreign Policy* by Jeffrey T. Bergner. It appeared in *American Politics.* Dr. Bergner explored the thesis that the Democrats were becoming isolationists and the Republicans internationalists. He traced this thesis in a rather sophisticated and subtle way.

Since this seemed an unusual and interesting line of argument, we got in touch with Jeff Bergner. Actually, we had talked with him earlier about the relationship between the president and Congress and how party alignment, for instance, affects this relationship. At the Miller Center we have tended to concentrate on the presidency, and yet the presidency operates within a constitutional system and not as some independent function. Dick Bolling emphasized this when he spoke about Congress and the presidency a few weeks ago. Jeff Bergner is going to look at it in terms of the challenges Congress poses to the presidency and the questions that this raises.

Jeffrey is part public servant, and part academician, which isn't a bad mix. He taught at Princeton, where he also received his M.A. and Ph.D. He received his undergraduate degree from Carleton College. He has taught at the University of Pennsylvania, the University of Michigan and Georgetown University. He has written a major work on the origins of formalism in social science, published by the University of Chicago Press. He published a number of articles on philosophy, politics, and economics which indicate the main direction of his interests such as: "Federal Spending Limitations: An Idea Whose Time Has

Come?"; "The Taiwan Relations Act"; "Does Development Assistance Have a Future?" and others. He served as staff director of the Senate Foreign Relations Committee and before that as Senator Richard Lugar's chief of staff. It is a pleasure to welcome him to the Center.

**MR. BERGNER:** Thank you. I very much appreciate the opportunity to be with you in this bastion of reason that Thomas Jefferson founded. This is all the more true because, as you may have heard, we are still practicing astrology in Washington.

As Ken pointed out, I would like to talk about the challenge to the presidency that comes from the Congress, and I'd like to identify several major areas in which the Congress is offering some new challenges to the presidency.

Let me put this in context by telling a little story that the President told the other day at the White House. The President has a hobby of collecting jokes Soviet citizens tell about their own system. On many occasions when he gives a talk, he tells one of these jokes. He told the story about a Soviet citizen who wanted to buy a new car. After this poor gentleman had saved up enough money, he finally went to buy a car. But first he had to go to one bureaucrat and talk to him about the procedures, and then was shuffled over to another office and yet another office. Finally, after being sent to about fifteen offices he came to the last bureaucrat in the line who said, "It appears that everything here is in order and you can buy the car. Your car won't be delivered for five years, but you have to pay for it up front." So the man counted out his rubles and said, "Will that car be delivered in the morning or the afternoon?" The bureaucrat asked, "Why on earth would it make any difference?" and the man said, "Well, the plumber is coming in the morning."

There are a lot of frustrations in dealing with that system. What I'd like to talk about today are some of the frustrations in dealing with our system. One assistant to the president for congressional relations at the State Department said, and I quote: "We can never seem to get anything done with the Congress. We have to testify over and over again to different committees and subcommittees in both the Senate and the House. We have to testify again and again on the smallest issues. It is like a floating crap game. There is nowhere to go to get a simple yes or no."

For the sake of organization, let me group the challenges and frustrations which the presidency confronts with the Congress into a couple of different categories, the first of which is the very broad structural challenges. Power in the Congress is now very widely dispersed. There is, as you know—and here I'm doing nothing other than repeating comments that many other people have made—no longer a congressional leadership structure for the president or his senior advisers to go to if they wish to make a deal with the Congress. There is no fixed set of interlocutors on any given issue. The number of people that become involved in various issues in the Congress is simply enormous. It has been estimated that in one particular year there were 163 different committees and subcommittees before which people had to testify in order to accomplish a single spending bill.

Also, you will see that there are no longer one or two places in the Senate and the House that deal exclusively with foreign affairs and national security issues. No longer can you talk only to the Armed Services Committee or the Foreign Relations Committee. Rather, every single committee has jurisdiction over something having to do with foreign affairs and national security. The Agriculture Committee has an input on trade negotiations with Japan which have now just broken down again; the Energy Committee is involved with Alaskan oil exports, Persian Gulf issues, and so forth. When I was the staff director of the Foreign Relations Committee, I felt this in a very visceral way, because from one day to the next people were encroaching on our territory. The president and his advisers on various occasions have to speak with almost every single person in the Senate and the House in order to get a foreign policy or national security question settled, and this makes the president's job a lot tougher.

At the same time, power and authority is very much dispersed within the executive branch as well. The executive branch has become a very large and complex organism. The executive branch tries to coordinate its policies by having Cabinet council meetings or interagency meetings at senior and not so senior levels, to try to

45

coordinate its policies. Consider, for example, a trade issue with Japan. On such an issue, a Cabinet council meeting includes the Treasury people, the Commerce people, the State Department people, Agriculture people, and it might include Defense people as well. There is the necessity of bringing these people together because the bureaucracy is so large and so dispersed.

This dispersion in the bureaucracy creates a set of natural alliances on the Hill. There is hardly ever an issue which hasn't been vented and decided upon in the executive branch first and then gets rehashed at the congressional level. The administration people who lost in the administration debate come right back to the Congress, find their allies there, and try to win in the Congress what they have just lost in the executive branch. And that happens again and again, whether it has to do with arms control or agriculture negotiations. Whatever the issue may be, from the ridiculous to the sublime, once the executive branch has arrived at a unified position, and has its troops in line, some of its people sneak around the back, as it were, and come to the Congress. They then provide willing people in the Congress, who want to fight this battle again, all sorts of information without which they couldn't really muster a very substantial case.

I wouldn't say that I was involved in this myself, of course, but the fact is that everybody is. You are looking for ammunition to build good arguments in fighting a legislative battle on a national security issue. You get that information from your allies in the executive branch, some of whom have won and some of whom have lost in a given instance.

You will often find that there are very severe disagreements within the executive branch. But when the president and his people have circled the wagons, it is much more difficult for the Congress to play a strong role on a national security issue. In short, the fact that power, information, and capacity is more widely dispersed, both in the Congress and the executive branch, makes it much more difficult for the president to get his way.

Secondly, over the last couple of decades the Congress has passed an enormous amount of legislation that restricts the president's capacity to act. I won't go through all of them, but beginning in the late 1960s and early 1970s, a series of these restrictions was enacted. Some are substantial and well known, such as the War Powers Resolution, the Arms Export Control Act, the Clark Amendment prohibiting shipment of arms to Angola (which subsequently has been repealed), and so on. The point I would make is this: even though there is a perception that President Reagan has rolled back a lot of the Congress' power in foreign affairs—and there are several instances in which that has been the case—in the Reagan years there was a substantial number of new restrictions placed on the president's power to act.

The reason a lot of these provisions have gotten through is that President Reagan has been reluctant to veto them. Reagan is a very tough talking President, but he vetoes just about nothing. If you think back on how many things this President has vetoed, there have not been very many. A lot of them come to him as big, fourteen pound bills of the continuing resolution kind that he threw down on the Speaker's desk when he made the State of the Union Address this year. It is very difficult, even if there are quibbles with certain restrictions in the bill, to veto the entire bill because of these small issues.

The fact that legislation comes in fewer pieces but with more parts, and the fact that this President has been reluctant to veto legislation, has led to the imposition of a substantial number of further restrictions on the President. With regard to different countries, all kinds of procedures must be enforced, all kinds of reports must be filed, and many kinds of limitations exist on sending individuals to a particular place. There are caps on the amount of money the president can spend to send people abroad. Indeed, many restrictions are imposed through the appropriations process.

The third thing I'd mention is that we have, to put it kindly, a very remarkable budget process. In fact, it is utterly ridiculous. It is redundant, unnecessary, and too complex. It forces the Congress to spend too much of its time revisiting issues which really don't need to be revisited as often as they are. There are, as you know, three levels to this process: there is the Budget Committee process in which the Budget Committee supposedly puts through the broad numbers in the beginning of the year; then there is the authorization process; and finally there is the appropriations process. The system is needlessly complex. And I would bet, although I hate to say this, that if you gave members of Congress a test asking them to tell you what is the precise difference between an authorization and an appropriation, many of them wouldn't know.

In order to get a dollar, the adminstration needs to go through three different processes: the budget process, the authorization process, and the appropriations process. This leads to Congress spending much of its time debating money issues rather than policy issues or reviewing how the money is spent—that is, oversight.

On national security and foreign policy issues this means that the administration and the Congress spend their time quibbling about whether they will spend more or less money on a given program rather than doing what the Congress really does best: looking at these programs from a distance and determining which ones are going well and which ones are not. In other words, Congress should be involved in a kind of leavening process. Instead, the Congress finds itself micromanaging and saying, "You've asked for $20 million for Zaire, but this year you are going to get only $12.5 million." After the administration loses the first round, it comes back and maybe gets $15 million. They spend the whole year on that exercise rather than looking at what it is we are trying to do with this money, and whether it is doing any good at all, regardless of whether $12.5, $15 or $20 million are spent. That's perhaps a little bit of an overstatement, but I think it is a fair assessment of the redundancy in the budgetary process.

Finally, I'd like to point to one other thing which is a little harder to define, something I call the "demystification" of foreign policy. When I first went to Washington on a Washington semester program in 1968, it was a very exciting spring there. A lot was going on that year. Even though the Congress was beginning to assert itself a little bit, I would basically describe the Congress as subservient. We talked to person after person who would say, "The President and his people have said such and such is the case. Who are we to argue with them?" I can very clearly recall this kind of deference to the president. This was just the

48

beginning of the period when that attitude changed. By the time we got to the early 1970s, it had changed with a vengeance.

Prior to the early 1970s, there was a sense that national security police was more mysterious and required a little bit more insider's knowledge than pork barrel politics and building bridges and dams. The quality of the people was a little bit different, too. There was a mystique about those who served in the foreign service. The Congress now regards foreign policy and national security as one more set of political choices which it needs to make, and involves itself as if these were domestic issues. The line between foreign and domestic policy has become totally blurred. As I said, there is no committee in the Congress that does not sometimes consider foreign policy issues. Congressmen and senators are much more at home in the area of foreign policy and no longer regard this as a preserve for a group of experts. They view the people in the executive branch who work in these fields as being very much like themselves: fallible and filled with ideas based on their own experiences.

I think this is a result, first, of the fact that a lot more congressmen and senators travel than was the case a generation or two ago. Many have served in the Peace Corps. For example, you can't tell Senator Dodd very much about the countries in which he served in the Peace Corps because he has been there. And quite a number of senators and congressmen have either had experiences in the Peace Corps, have studied abroad, or traveled abroad.

Secondly, the information available to Congress these days is much greater. Twenty or thirty years ago, during the time when Eisenhower was considering his actions with regard to Lebanon, most people didn't know where Lebanon was. Today everybody knows where it is. You see it on the news practically every night. So the access to information is much greater.

Also, the Congress now has a substantial staff in place. If there is a single congressional reform which needs to be carried out, it should be, in my mind at least, to reduce the congressional staff. The congressional staff is a very energetic group of people, and by and large they have a lot of ideas, and have been to a lot of places. Many of them used to work in the administration at some point or are on leave from the administration on various programs. This group provides considerable expertise, making it a far more equal struggle between the two branches on foreign policy issues.

And finally, the number of constituents in a given congressman's or senator's district or state that are somehow touched by foreign policy or by trade matters is much higher now than it was. Two decades ago 3 or 4 percent of the population depended for its livelihood on jobs that had to do with exports or imports. Now the number may be four times that high, maybe 16 percent. BMW, Mercedes, or Japanese car dealers, people that sell agricultural commodities abroad, or the steel workers and television manufacturers who feel threatened by imports, all have a stake in foreign policy issues. Foreign policy issues and national security issues have become a matter of constituent politics to a greater extent than they were before.

When I was in Senator Lugar's office, about half of the mail we received in any given week, however many thousand letters that was, probably had something to do with foreign policy or foreign trade in a broad sense. When that is the case, you can be sure that members of Congress, who are very sensitive to public pressure, are not going to simply stand back and leave this province to someone else. Quite to the contrary, for all of these reasons you will find the Congress continually and perhaps increasingly involved in foreign trade and foreign policy questions. There is a kind of new internationalism—not in that mushy old U.N. sense, but in a very real, tangible, economic sense. Substantial constituencies for and against restrictions on foreign trade have emerged and have made Congress more responsive to their concerns.

All of these are changes in the broad structure of procedures and interests in the Congress. They suggest that the Congress is simply not going to be deferential to the president any longer and is going to make his life much more interesting when it comes to foreign policy or national security decisions.

The second area I'd like to talk about briefly is the

change that has taken place in the substance of views that people in this country and in the Congress hold. Think back twenty-five years, and try to answer the following questions. Which party is the party of internationalism? Which party is the party of free trade? Which party is the party that favors closer relations with Europe and our allies? Which seeks broader involvement in world affairs and favors more foreign assistance, not less? I don't think there is much doubt that the answer to any of these questions would have been the Democratic Party.

Today, although it is not widely acknowledged, if you answer those questions honestly, you would have to say that there is a far greater natural reservoir of support for many of those issues in the Republican Party. There has been a shift in attitudes between the parties which makes it difficult for people to orient themselves. The Republican Party is clearly more in favor of free trade than the Democratic Party at this point. The Republican Party quibbles far less about our relationship with the NATO allies. The Republican Party quibbles far less about the projection of power anywhere in the world than does the Democratic Party.

Look, for example, at the Persian Gulf. When Jimmy Carter was the Democratic President, he enunciated the Carter Doctrine to assert America's vital interest in the Persian Gulf. We didn't have twenty Republicans stand up and disagree with him about that. Indeed, people wondered privately whether he meant it, and whether he was going to make it stick or not. But then the Democrats just left it at that. Now a Republican President enforces the Carter Doctrine and sends ships to escort foreign vessels. And now we find a good bit of public criticism and concern on the part of the Democratic Party.

In a way, the situation has turned upside down. The kind of people who made up the core of the Republican party back in the 1920s and 1930s, the bankers and farmers, are now international in orientation. And the labor unions, which used to be international in the sense of feeling some solidarity with other labor unions, or at least opposing people who were suppressing free labor unions, have turned in on themselves and become concerned with protecting what they have. They have adopted a much more defensive strategy. This shift became quite clear to me last year when we found the President threatening to veto the Democrats' foreign assistance bill because it was too small. This is President Reagan.

But it is not just that the parties simply changed roles. Over and above that, there has been a breakdown in the kind of bipartisanship which existed in the decades after World War II. It's not just a shift of parties, in other words, in which one assumes the role of the other; there are some features that are qualitatively new. There was a broad agreement for twenty years or so about the essence of American foreign policy. People called it "bipartisanship" sometimes, but what it meant was containment. There was a bipartisan agreement that containment was the core, the essence, the key to our foreign policy, and it was clear that containment was not just a goal but that it also specified some means on how to put that policy into practice.

Although containment is still intact when it comes to the central theater, that is, Europe, NATO, and the Warsaw Pact, or the central questions regarding strategic weapons, and while there is still a broad bipartisan agreement on the core aspects of containment, there have been changes. What is new and different is that there is now no agreement whatsoever on containment when it comes to outlying areas in the world. There is simply no bipartisan agreement on that at all. Agreement has broken down on how to implement containment with regard to the low-intensity conflicts, as they are called, in Nicaragua or Angola, for example. Here fundamental differences between the two parties have developed, though it took some time for this to occur.

It was in some ways the result of the Democratic Party's experience with the Vietnam War. It turned in a direction away from foreign involvement, and the first manifestation of that was Jimmy Carter. I can remember very clearly various stages in this development in the late 1970s, and in fact was involved in one of them. Up until 1979 there was a bipartisan or nonpartisan staff, if you will, on the Foreign Relations Committee. In 1979 that changed and there were partisan staffs, a Republican or a minority staff, and a Democratic or majority staff. At the time the Republicans insisted on this; they were the agents of this break, while the Democrats were very reluctant to create a partisan staff in the Senate Foreign Relations Committee. The Republicans ended up doing it anyway for one very simple reason: in their view, the call for bipartisanship simply meant doing things the way the Democrats wanted to do it. It didn't really mean reaching out for consensus. In the late 1970s you began to see a substantial split of opinion about how to deal with power projection abroad or how to apply force, how to deal with the resistance movements to communist governments, or whether that was even all that important in some of these outlying areas. It is perfectly clear that disagreement continues right down to this day. That has not been smoothed over.

For example, when you hear Michael Dukakis say that perhaps we should look at removing troops from South Korea, you realize that nothing has changed very much. I just hope for his sake that he finds some advisers who can recall for him the experience that Jimmy Carter had when he made that same proposal, which did not work out very well and ended up being withdrawn.

It is very clear that the hearts of the two parties are in different places on the issue of containment, freedom fighters, rollback, or whatever term you want to use. There is disagreement on whether these areas are important, whether there are other or more useful options than the use of force, and under what circumstances you should intervene militarily. And if you look at the points where the Congress has tried to assert itself most forcefully, it always turns out to be on the issue of how to deal with containment on the perimeter. That is exactly what the War Powers Act is about: let's not have another Vietnam without coming back to the Congress as the arbiter. Similarly, the Arms Export Control Act says: don't send arms abroad—especially to the Middle East—unless Congress gives approval to do that. On nuclear nonproliferation, the same kind of legislative veto approach was put into effect in the 1970s. Restrictions were imposed on the number of U.S. advisers in El Salvador. Other restrictions were imposed on what can be done in a particular country as with the Clark Amendment in Angola.

That's really the flash point for all of these problems between the executive and the legislative: the question of how to address regional or low-intensity conflict. This is not just a structural problem, but a real change of view and a real national disagreement about how to proceed. It is also something which will cause problems for any president—for President Bush if he wishes to get further involved in Nicaragua or for President Dukakis if he wishes to become less entangled. This is going to be a problem for either one of them. There is simply no doubt about it.

Let me now identify a third set of challenges that will come to any president from the Congress in foreign policy and national security. Aside from the structural challenges and substantive differences, I also think that the type of people who serve in the Congress now are a little bit different from those who served before. This is difficult to talk about, and I don't mean to be unfair or unrealistic or to look longingly to a different day, so let me state this in a tentative fashion.

It seems to me that we have seen a very real democratization of the Senate and the House, producing a more independent type of congressman. These are self-made individuals, who come to the Senate and the House with no obligation to anybody. They raise their own money; they have their own press operation; they are dependent upon no one but themselves. They are free spirits. They don't come by virtue of long service to a state party structure where they have served with the leaders of the state party. Consequently, they haven't had their edges rounded off by consensus and accommodation and by having to exercise leadership roles in the states from which they've come. They are much more individualistic. I'm not saying this is bad; I am simply saying the situation is different.

The old kinds of understandings, the common ties that once existed in terms of outlook or even in terms of what schools people had attended, have pretty much disappeared. Senators and congressman are different now. Many come from places nobody has ever heard of or from schools nobody has ever gone to; they are self-made people. They've set up their own organizations, and they are going to be reelected by themselves, too. They rely not one whit on the state party. In some cases they have their own organizations in every county of their states or districts which simply mirror the state organization. They are a very different kind of people, who really are not very much inclined to look on the president in an accommodating way. The president, to these members, is just one more fellow who has his own views, just as they have theirs.

At the risk of really going out on a limb, I want to say one more thing about that, and that is in some ways the president has become like that too; and I mean not only this President, but presidents in recent times. There is a world of difference between a Franklin Roosevelt, on the one hand, and a Jimmy Carter, a Ronald Reagan, or a Mike Dukakis, on the other. Presidents really come from all kinds of places now too; they have held all kinds of jobs and done all kinds of things. They, too, are beholden to no one when they come to power. Look at Jimmy Carter, Ronald Reagan, or Mike Dukakis. They had their own organizations, created sometimes over and against the national party organization. They raised their own money, had their own staff, did their own media work, and knew that they didn't have to answer to anybody. Sometimes when they come into office, as Jimmy Carter did, they assume that this will continue to be the case, and that the Congress is going to be mightily impressed by that, which is a very bad mistake, because Congress is not.

President Nixon, in his book called *1999: Victory Without War*, says at one point that in order to respond to the crafty Gorbachev and the new challenges we face in the Soviet Union, we will need a very strong effort from what he calls "the American leadership class." I'm not sure that there is such a thing anymore. In his review of Nixon's book, Bob Ellsworth, who served as Senator Dole's presidential campaign manager, said—and I quote him because I think it is interesting—"The existence of an 'American leadership class' is an unconfirmed conjecture." If it ever existed, it is not so clear that one exists any more. In its place, he maintains, you have an ever shifting group of winners and losers with very little that binds them together.

When Nixon came up into the political system, there still was a leadership class, and he wanted to be part of it. One could tell that from the enormous resentment he harbored against certain people born into it. It seems there really was a group of people who crossed party lines, and had a great deal to say about what this country would do and how it would be run.

But younger people who come into the system now see the Nixons and the Carters simply as people who happen to be president. They don't see a leadership class any more. There really is only a group of shifting winners and losers, and it is not clear what their common ties are. It is not clear that a Dukakis and a Nixon have one single thing in common that would ever lead them to talk to one another ten years down the road if Dukakis were to become president. In effect, I am saying that we have democratized our country in a remarkably successful way. If every first-time congressman, no matter how inexperienced he is and how little he has thought about national security or foreign policy matters, thinks that his views are just as good as the president's, that's what democracy is all about. That's why I chose in the beginning to speak about challenges to the presidency, not challenges to the president. The challenges to the presidency come from a lot of different quarters, including sometimes from the presidents themselves, who may invite the kind of challenges and confrontations which they so unhappily experience.

This brings me back to the beginning where I talked a little bit about the frustrations that senior officials or presidents feel in dealing with the Congress. These frustrations have many origins: structural and procedural changes, substantive changes in viewpoints of the world and our role in it, and also, I think, the different kinds of people who increasingly occupy the offices in the Congress and the presidency. Some of the old forms of reverence for the country's institutions are no longer quite so significant as they once were.

It has often been said that American businesses have too short a time horizon. They are not looking far enough into the future for the good of the corporation. Their attention is fixed on the next quarter's earnings so they can project how big their bonus is going to be or how their performance is going to be measured. I don't know if that is true or not. I'm not a student of the history of American business. But I would say that this is true, in spades, of the American political leadership which we now have. Their time horizon has become very compact, and a successful policy is not one whose results can be measured in decades or years, but in weeks, or days, or even hours in some cases.

But some of our problems don't really admit to such rapid solutions. Negotiating a reasonable arms control agreement, resolving the federal deficit problem or figuring out what to do about strategic defense and the right mix of offensive and defensive strategic forces are not problems to tackle in a day or a week. But you increasingly find politicians whose time horizons are such that they need to justify success or failure within a very short time frame. They comment on something one day and go on to the next press release the following day.

We find ourselves in a situation in which the Congress will continue to offer challenges to the presidency regardless of whether the president is a Republican or a Democrat; whether he thinks well of Congress or thinks the Congress is part of the problem; whether he has views that are internationalist or isolationist; and whether he is for or against the use of force abroad. I see no surcease from these challenges to the presidency. The office, as described in Article II of the Constitution, has the same powers and authorities that it has always had. But in reality those powers will be either greater or smaller depending on the quality of the individual who occupies the office and the talent of those who are attempting to limit his power. I think we are fated to see rather intense congressional-presidential confrontations in foreign policy for many years to come. And on that somewhat rainy note on this somewhat rainy day, I will end.

**NARRATOR:** The person who deserves credit for this very stimulating discussion is my assistant, Peter Tester, who kept reminding me to write a letter of invitation to Jeff Bergner. He ought to have the right to the first question.

**QUESTION:** My question has to do with the last topic you touched upon, the compact time frame that legislators have. For example, with regard to most favored nation status toward Romania, which was originally granted when the conditions for emigration were vastly different, how is this legislation reviewed? Is it reviewed by the staff in terms of a deterioration of human rights, say? Or is that something that senators do?

**MR. BERGNER:** Let me begin by saying that the executive branch doesn't review these things at all. They don't like these restrictions, they never have, and they never will. If the State Department is compelled to do something, it will do it as little as possible and process it as slowly as possible. If something is to be reviewed, it has to be forced out on the agenda by the Hill, and that's the view of the Hill.

In the case of Romania, Senator Helms was successful in helping to secure the appointment of Dave Funderberk, the ambassador to Romania for the Reagan administration. Funderberk was a professor from North Carolina and very conservative. He went over to Romania and, unlike other ambassadors, who often end up getting along perhaps a little too well with the people they deal with, he didn't like their government much. He thought that the Romanian government was a very rough bunch of people. He had nothing good to say about them, and ended up providing a very negative view to the Hill about the situation in Romania. That led to a lot of discussions on the Senate and House floors about Romania. Funderberk is not there any longer, as someone else has come in to fill that spot, but the discussion continues.

How are these things done by and large? I think the Romanian incident is very typical of the way things happen. If there are people on the Hill who have good relationships with someone in the ambassador's office or someone unseen who is able to provide reliable background information, that is wonderful material for Congress. After all, this was debated in the White House interagency group, the NSC and State, and yet nothing was done about it.

In short, I think there generally is not a systematic review of these things. The executive branch doesn't want to do it, and Congress isn't informed enough to do it. It is done on a case by case basis by the Congress or some set of individuals in Congress who initiate this activity.

Knowledge really is power; if you don't know anything, you are not going to have any power. But if you scratch long enough for information you will invariably find people in the administration who are willing to help.

QUESTION: You painted a rather bleak picture of the long-range planning in our country. I'd like to ask who you think should be doing that? The obvious answer is everybody. But is there any particular institution that you are looking at?

MR. BERGNER: The urgent replaces the important in every walk of life, and that's pretty much what happens in the government, too. You may have a meeting to try to figure out what should be done now about the beef negotiations with Japan because these guys are recalcitrant. Do we offer them something in return? Do we take a five year phaseout? Since you have to discuss that, it is very hard to step back and find time to reflect on what our overall relations with Japan should be like. What trends should we be encouraging and what not?

There is a clearly felt need for that sort of planning, so much so that a couple of years back the National Security Council began to bring some people together for the purpose of long-range planning. That process was cut off in mid-spring for a variety of reasons, including the unfortunate death of one of the people who was most motivated to do this. That is certainly one locus for long-term planning because it cuts across departmental and agency boundaries. I think that the Congress, it if were doing what it does best, would be a very good place to do that, too. Let the executive branch deal with the day-to-day things, and let the Congress review policy, conduct oversight, and offer general guidance for planning.

While he was chairman of the Foreign Relations Committee, Senator Church got involved in this process and was beginning to do some very excellent work reviewing U.S. policy toward Southwest Asia regarding energy and strategic interests. Right in the middle of it the hostage crisis came up and his project was totally overtaken by events. We had hundreds of briefings about what was going on day by day. Church's approach, nevertheless, is the kind of thing the Congress can do very well. It can step back, take a broader look, and force the administration to take a broader look. Instead, the Congress has for the most part focused in recent years on micromanaging programs; that is, decide how much foreign aid a particular country should get, or how much foreign military assistance. How much of that should be in grants and how much in loans. What conditions should be attached to the aid, and that sort of thing. There are too many endless debates about numbers.

There have been, however, two or three fairly substantial efforts in the Congress to take the long view, and they have been very useful exercises. Senator Jackson certainly did that in the early 1960s; Senator Nunn is doing a little bit of that in a series of hearings he is holding now. It can be done. I think the National Security Council is a good place to do some of this work but they are also inevitably overcome by day-to-day events. There is a State Department policy planning staff as well. The problem you always run into, is that people who are planning policies, but are not involved in day-to-day activities, aren't taken with sufficient seriousness by people who are involved in day-to-day problems. How you integrate planning and action remains a very significant problem. The National Security Council and the Congress are two likely centers of whatever long-term planning can be done.

QUESTION: You concluded your remarks by saying you didn't see any surcease—I believe that was your word—from a situation which strikes me as being quite the norm in American history; that is, the situation of diffused power and maximum participation in policy, and the non-existence of a unified leadership class. Do you see any virtues or strengths in this that you might not find in the continuation of a strong presidential system of the Roosevelt crisis management variety?

MR. BERGNER: Yes. I'm glad you asked that because I didn't mean to paint an altogether negative picture, or leave the impression that I'm anti-democratic. I think there are enormous virtues in it. There are certainly a substantial number of people interested and involved in foreign policy and national security questions that were never involved before. In some cases, these people make important contributions, and we get involved in different issues than we might otherwise.

We often have significant debates about the morality of our policies. Broad participation helps carry that element into foreign policy which has been important throughout American history. We've never been a country wholly satisfied with *realpolitik*, that is a foreign policy based on calculations of strength, balancing one actor against another. The many black Americans involved in debates about our South Africa policy, a big lobby involved in our policy toward Greece, Turkey, and Cyprus, or AIPAC, and other Jewish lobby groups trying to influence our Middle East policy, help to integrate a kind of human dimension into calculations of power politics. I think that's a good thing for this country because we would never be capable of conducting a policy on the basis of calculation of power alone. That's just not the kind of country, the kind of people, or the kind of tradition we have. There is a great deal to be said for a fuller involvement in foreign policy by many new people, and many new actors. It certainly sensitizes this country to a lot of things which might not be a part of our foreign policy otherwise.

**COMMENT:** Specifically with respect to the Congress, you might not get a senator like Richard Lugar, who has independent competence as well as expertise, in an old-style Rooseveltian system. You might not get a senator like Nunn; you might not get those legislators who become specialists in policy if they weren't playing a wider participatory role.

**MR. BERGNER:** That could be. I might dissent a little bit from that. There have been great legislators throughout our country's history. After all, the Congress has been one important place from which presidents have been drawn. How to get a system in which competence is rewarded and given due weight is really the problem we confront. So I'm not sure I would agree wholly that we now have a group of legislators who are stronger and qualitatively better than before.

A while back I talked to a group of people interested in foreign assistance, a group very much on the liberal side of the spectrum. We talked about what was involved in the process of democratization and how it could best be promoted. These people were very much concerned about giving more foreign assistance to the poor to promote development and democratization. At the same time, this group favored a more democratic and participatory approach in American government decision-making. I made the point that the more democratic the system becomes and the more people's views are taken into account, the less foreign aid is likely to be given. If you constructed a tax system which was perfectly democratic, namely, one in which each of us could write down what he wanted his own tax to be spent on each year, you would probably get money for defense and repairing the roads, but you'd probably have a very small foreign aid budget, much smaller than we have now. The protectors of foreign aid have been people with a broader vision, people who have had a sense of *noblesse oblige*. The Jacob Javits and the Hubert Humphreys of the world are people who look out for these things, despite the fact that there is no earthly domestic political reason to do so. These kinds of people have always come up in the system. My concern is that although they still exist, there are many more people with a short-term outlook. They are politicians who look only toward the next election.

QUESTION: I'd like to ask a follow-up question to that. I wonder if the rise of the power of the individual congressman may not have narrowed rather than broadened the democratic base. The power of the PACs and the influence each individual congressman can get without going back to the political system, as I see it, really narrows the breadth of his interest. He becomes a creature of the relatively few groups by which he might be supported.

MR. BERGNER: I'm going to offer another view, though there may be something to what you say. Madison once said, when talking about the difference between the House and Senate, that the more democratic the machine looks by virtue of the greater number of people involved in it, the fewer secret springs there are which really animate its activities. Sometimes things appear very democratic when you have large numbers of people involved, but that really may narrow the number of people who are making the genuine decisions about what is on the agenda and how these things will work out.

There are so many PACs now and so much political money that they almost neutralize each other. I know because I'm beat upon mercilessly for contributions every day in my current line of work. In the days when someone was able to give a quarter of a million dollars to a campaign and that would constitute 50 percent of all the money raised, that person probably had pretty good access to the candidate and a pretty good relationship. Now, in a campaign that raises $3 million and the limit for a PAC contribution is $5,000, or for an individual $1,000 or $2,000, there will be a lot of $2,000 to $5,000 givers. There will be even more who have given less than that through direct mail solicitations. It is true that there is an enormous amount of money in the system, but it may be coming from a more diverse base.

There may be something to what you say, although my experience tells me something else. When I ran a Senate staff and some guy came in from a PAC that gave $5,000, my reaction was pleasant and polite, as I always try to be, but so what? He was one of a large crowd of contributors. In a way, contributing doesn't buy you any more than if you didn't; namely, a polite, sympathetic hearing, to the extent that you can be sympathetic. To the extent that you cannot be accommodating, you are not going to be.

In short, I think that the evils of PAC funding have been greatly overstated, although in fairness, there is a lot of money washing through the system now.

QUESTION: Aren't the different roles of Congress and the executive branch which you referred to in your presentation a cyclical phenomenon which has been going on since Madison's time? If you look back over the presidency from 1960 to at least part of the Reagan presidency, there seems to have been a latent instability. Don't you think Congress is really filling the vacuum that this latent instability of the presidency has created?

MR. BERGNER: Yes, I think so. You can find times when there were very strong partisan differences between the parties, as with our policy regarding England and France early in this country's history. There was less bipartisanship then than there is now. You can also point to times when the Congress literally rode roughshod over the president, as in the post-Civil War period. There were times when the committee chairmen didn't want to tell the president what was going on. I do believe this is a kind of phenomenon that comes and goes.

I guess what makes this cycle appear so marked is that most people who are now running our system grew up in a period of post-World War II bipartisanship. The present period looks very different measured against that benchmark which lasted roughly from 1945 to 1965. I was not trying to suggest that this is a brand new phenomena. I do think, however, that some of the things I mentioned, namely, the internationalization of our economy and our life, and the kind of people that fill some of these offices now, are new and different phenomena. But you can certainly trace a cyclical pattern in the history of legislative-executive relations. Arthur Schlesinger wrote a good article that made that point.

**COMMENT:** He has changed his mind now.

**MR. BERGNER:** Well, he has changed mine, too. All these fans of the imperial presidency in the Roosevelt years decided they really didn't like it too much when Nixon got there.

**NARRATOR:** His father's essay on this subject was even better than his. But that is going way back.

**QUESTION:** Do you think foreign policy will have a more important influence in this election [1988] than in previous elections?

**MR. BERGNER:** No, I don't. I would say that at the level of presidential elections there are only a couple of issues that are ever decisive. One is whether the economy is doing well or not. The economy is doing well at the moment. We are borrowing endlessly to make it do well, but that's the compromise everybody has agreed on—the "no pain" approach. We won't cut spending, we won't cut defense, and we won't raise taxes; we will just borrow the money. But the economy, apart from that, is doing pretty well. Unemployment today is the lowest it has been in fourteen years. That's likely to be the principal issue in a presidential campaign.

If it turns out that the country is doing reasonably well, George Bush will probably want to stress that, and there may be less to run on if you are a Democrat. Dukakis will have to try to find something else to run on, but foreign policy may be a little tough for him to run on. George Bush is busy trying to monopolize that.

Rather than foreign policy, a feeling of national security and national strength can become an election issue. But I don't really think it is going to be any more of an issue than it was, say, in 1984. In 1980 it was a rather substantial issue because of the Iran hostage crisis and the sense that things were slipping away from us abroad. In short, foreign policy will be no more an issue than is usually the case, and less so than has been the case in years like 1980, for example.

**NARRATOR:** There are some things that would be interesting to pursue further, such as the fact that on the containment issue there was a good deal of difference between the views of Marshall, Bohlen, Kennan, and others. Even Acheson wasn't very happy with the allocation of funds to China. No one was ready to go quite as far with Taiwan as Senator Knowland was. There were these differences, though, and maybe they will be the subject of our next forum with Jeffrey Bergner. We look forward to continuing our relationship with him.

# IV. The Supreme Court and the Presidency

## JUSTICE LEWIS F. POWELL

MR. JORDAN: On behalf of the staff and the trustees of the Thomas Jefferson Memorial Foundation, I am pleased to welcome you to our first program in the 1988 series of Conversations at Monticello. While we always enjoy working with Ken Thompson and the Miller Center, this evening is special, because we have with us the most distinguished lawyer and jurist from Virginia since the glory days of the great generation of Jefferson, John Marshall, Patrick Henry, and more Randolphs than we could name. Introducing our speaker tonight is Kenneth W. Thompson, director of the White Burkett Miller Center of Public Affairs at the University of Virginia.

NARRATOR: If this event is a high point for Monticello, it is to no less a degree a high moment for the Miller Center, both with regard to the man and his legend that links up so closely, I think, with the legends of presidents which the Center addresses. The man, all of you know, is among Virginia's greatest legal minds and his beginnings are no less Virginian. He was born in Suffolk, educated at Washington and Lee, graduated with both arts and science degrees and law degrees as well as with an LL.M. from Harvard. He was admitted to the Bar of Virginia in 1931, and to the U.S. Supreme Court bar in 1937. He was named Associate Justice of the Supreme Court in 1972.

What all may not know are some of his varied and distinctive achievements such as a war record which is second to none. He spent thirty-three months overseas, and received the Bronze Star Medal, the Croix de Guerre with

Palms from France and the Legion of Merit. His recognition by the legal profession is equally impressive with such honors as Honorary Bencher of Lincoln's Inn, Fellow of the American Bar Foundation, as well as appointment to a number of other important offices. But the legend is even more impressive in many respects, and I thought of it as I read a passage this morning from Daniel Webster because it seems to summarize that legend:

> If the blessings of our political and social condition have been too highly esteemed, we cannot well overrate the responsibility and duty which they impose upon us. We hold these institutions of government, religion, and learning to be transmitted as well as enjoyed. We are in the line of conveyance through which whatever has been obtained by the spirit and efforts of our ancestors is to be communicated to our children.

It is a very great privilege for the Miller Center to welcome Virginia's Associate Justice of the Supreme Court, Mr. Lewis F. Powell.

**JUSTICE POWELL:** Thank you very much, Ken, Mr. Director, ladies and gentlemen. It is a privilege to take part in one of these discussions. As a matter of fact, I didn't even know about them until I had a briefing from Dick Merrill, but they certainly sound like very interesting occasions. Of course the setting is unique. It is always very moving to be here. One of the great experiences I had was back in the presidency of Jerry Ford when on the lawn behind me over a hundred aliens were sworn in as American citizens. I'll always recall with admiration that Jerry Ford stood just inside that door and shook hands with every single one of them. It was a joy to watch the expressions of the faces of those new citizens as they shook hands with the President of the United States.

In reading the booklet of the activities of the Miller Center, I was much impressed with the scope and depth of what the Center is doing and what it has already accomplished. I notice that the basic purpose is to study and perhaps improve the presidency, and the focus of many

68

of the Center's activities has been in that direction. Speaking as a lawyer and a judge, I suppose the first thing that I think about in terms of the presidency is the president's critical role in nominating persons to serve on federal courts, and particularly the United States Supreme Court. We've gone through one such experience fairly recently and have seen the controversy it may provoke. Therefore the emphasis on its importance is fairly obvious to all of us. Yet even so I'll say a few words about that.

The history books record that about 20 percent of the persons nominated for the United States Supreme Court by the president have been rejected by the Senate, some perhaps for just cause. But I could name more than one who, in my opinion, were rejected by the Senate for causes that were less than just. Nevertheless, the Constitution provides for confirmation by the Senate, and so the Senate as a whole and the Judiciary Committee in particular have a major responsibility.

Still, the nomination is made by the president, and I think there have been times when the president of the United States has perhaps not been as careful in selecting the persons to be nominated to the Court as would be desirable. It may be a subject for further study as to the extent to which careful investigations of nominees to the Court have been made. It is fairly typical to have the FBI find out whether you have a criminal record, but that's minor compared to other considerations that may be pertinent to service on the Supreme Court.

I think it is important to keep in mind that the U.S. judicial branch of government is unique among the countries of the world. There are some other countries that appear to follow our example in form, but in fact only the U.S. Supreme Court specifically has authority as an independent branch of government. Other courts do not have the final authority "to decide what the law is," as John Marshall ruled in *Marbury vs. Madison*. Even in Great Britain, from which we've taken so much of our legal system, the top judiciary there, the House of Lords sitting as a Court, can be overruled by the House of Commons. What I've just said accents the importance of the president's role in nominating, not only members of the Supreme Court, but members of the entire federal judiciary.

# THE SUPREME COURT AND THE PRESIDENCY

I thought it might be appropriate, in light of what has happened in recent months [the Senate's rejection of Judge Robert Bork as Supreme Court associate justice] to talk a little bit about what I call the "new Supreme Court". On a court with only nine members and on which all nine sit on every case, the change of a single member of that court can sometimes have a profound effect. In the past two years there have been significant changes about which I will briefly refresh your memory.

In June 1986 Chief Justice Burger retired from the Court to assume the chairmanship of the Bicentennial Commission. I think it is fair to say that he has been a superb chairman of that commission. He has done a great many innovative things. I'll just cite a couple of them that may amuse you. I'm told that he has arranged for the napkins and placemats in every McDonald's restaurant in the United States to have something about the Constitution printed on them and to change the theme every month. He has done the same thing with Post cereal boxes. On a more scholarly level, he resurrected Catherine Drinker Bowen's *Miracle at Philadelphia: The Story of the Constitutional Convention*, which had been out of print for fifteen or twenty years. He had it reprinted in paperback, and he wrote an introduction to it. I think that Warren Burger, although many wondered why he was willing to give up the chief justiceship, quite sincerely felt that it was more important to celebrate the bicentennial appropriately, and he has done it magnificently.

You may be interested to know that none of the other justices, with the exception of Bill Rehnquist, had any inkling that Warren Burger was going to retire. I was taking a nap in my chambers, as I was then instructed to do by my physicians, when there was a knock on my door and a messenger told me that the chief justice wanted us in the conference room. It was about five minutes to 2 o'clock when I arrived in the conference room. There was a television set in there and others were gathering. The White House was shown on television and the President announced that Chief Justice Burger was retiring, and that he was appointing Justice Rehnquist as Chief Justice of the United States, and Judge Scalia as an associate justice. That was a very significant change in the history of the

70

Supreme Court and perhaps in our country. It reflects the degree of responsibility of the president.

Most of you know a good deal about Antonin Scalia because he taught on the faculty of the University of Virginia Law School. He graduated *magna cum laude* from Harvard Law School, which is not easy to do. He practiced briefly and also taught at the University of Chicago and Stanford. He brought to the Court a level of scholarship that was a credit to the President. I think Justice Scalia will make his mark on the Court. Nino, as we call him, does ask counsel more questions than any other justice. We have had fun reminding Nino that he was on the Supreme Court bench and not in the classroom.

I retired on 26 June 1987. At age 80, and in view of health problems, I thought the time had come for me. I do miss the Court. I did not anticipate the difficulty that occurred in replacing me.

When Bill Douglas retired, John Stevens was appointed, promptly confirmed, and sat on the Court at the beginning of the new term. In other words, he sat throughout the whole term. The same thing happened when Potter Stewart retired and Justice O'Connor was appointed in his place. She was nominated and confirmed and sat on the first Monday in October. This also occurred when then Judge Scalia was nominated and confirmed; he had time to prepare for the October session. When the replacement is not appointed and confirmed promptly, the Court is handicapped operating with only eight members. Many of the cases are extremely difficult. The questions that come to the Court often involve major issues of constitutional law. When only eight justices are sitting, the Court often splits four to four. That's a disservice to all concerned, particularly to the litigants. Yet this has happened in the current term because of the delay in filling my vacancy.

Finally Justice Kennedy was confirmed. I am happy to say that I think he is an excellent appointment. He is a graduate of Stanford University and Harvard Law School; he practiced law in Sacramento in a good law firm that gave him a broad experience at the bar. He also taught constitutional law over a period of some years at the McGeorge School of Law at the University of the Pacific, which will no doubt help him on the Supreme Court. As

71

you know, he was a judge on the Ninth Circuit when he was nominated. Since I had never met him until he came to the Court, I was surprised to find that he looks like a basketball player. He is about 6 feet, 3 inches tall and is very warm and gracious. Justices who have sat with him at the first session have all complimented him on the way he conducted himself. So the choice of Kennedy is an example of a President making an excellent nomination. Now, in effect, we have a new Court, and a strong one.

Of course, the president of the United States has very broad responsibilities. Few rank in importance with the authority he has to nominate persons for the federal judiciary, and particularly the United States Supreme Court.

Now I might stop at this point, Mr. Thompson, if that's appropriate.

**NARRATOR:** Who would like to begin our conversation with Justice Powell?

**QUESTION:** Justice Powell, a good deal of concern has been expressed about the increasing workload of the Court. Do you think this is a serious problem, and if so, do you have suggestions for its alleviation?

**JUSTICE POWELL:** It is a serious problem. I don't remember the exact statistics, but as of now in a typical year—and this has been true for the last half a dozen years or so—we have more than 4,000 petitions for *certiorari*, or appeals. One of the important duties of the Court is selecting the cases that are important enough for us to review.

The last term I was on the Court we granted about 175 of the 4,000 cases that were filed with us. The task of screening these requires the assistance of law clerks, but in the end Justices must vote on those cases. Happily, in this connection, most are criminal case petitions. About 60 to 65 percent of the petitioners are filed on behalf of criminal defendants. If one is appointed to defend a party charged with a crime, or if a lawyer is privately engaged to do so, and loses the case, the defendant often thinks that he had "ineffective assistance" of counsel. He then may insist that his lawyer—or a new lawyer—file a petition with the United

72

States Court of Appeals, and finally with a United States Supreme Court. Of course, if the defendant loses, the lawyer—however diligent—has been "ineffective." At any rate, the great majority of criminal appeals are frivolous. Therefore, the difficulty in dealing with them is not as great as the sheer mass would indicate.

The great majority of cases come to the Court on petitions for *certiorari*. Our jurisdiction as to these is discretionary. But the Court also has appellate jurisdiction to review decisions of state supreme courts that involve constitutional issues. These are not discretionary.

The second part of your question is what can be done to alleviate our workload. Congress has not been helpful in this respect. For years the Court has hoped its appellate jurisdiction also would be made discretionary. Chief Justice Burger proposed that a special court be created to review certain types of cases decided by courts of appeal. This court would be composed of judges serving on courts of appeals. These judges would come to Washington to sit on this special court on a rotating basis. Its primary duty would be to rule on petitions that involved conflicts between circuits. In some terms of our Court 25 to 30 percent of the cases have been granted to resolve conflict between various circuits. For example, all of us in Virginia live in the 4th Circuit. If the 4th Circuit Court of Appeals decides a tax question differently from the 9th Circuit Court of Appeals, we might be paying more taxes in Virginia than citizens in California. That's a condition that Virginia shouldn't tolerate. Invariably, we review that sort of case, and sometimes the issue is not easy to decide because excellent Courts of Appeals in different circuits have reached very different results.

The Burger proposal was that, since we had almost a compelling duty to take those cases, this new court should at least be given a five-year trial period. But judges on the Court of Appeals didn't like the idea, and you can understand why. They now rank second in the hierarchy: there are District Court judges, Court of Appeals judges, and Supreme Court justices. If the Burger plan has been approved—and it is still on the back burner—it would have meant that, at least for a period of time, there would be four levels of federal courts.

Dating back for many years federal courts, pursuant to a federal statute, have had jurisdiction over cases involving citizens of different states. This no longer makes sense, and Congress could substantially relieve the workload of all federal courts by abolishing diversity jurisdiction.

QUESTION: As you are the godfather of our American Bar Committee on Law and National Security, could you tell us how it got started when you were serving on the school board of the City of Richmond, and why you thought there was a vacuum in education and teaching in this country about our basic doctrines in contrast with communist doctrine?

JUSTICE POWELL: The question was asked by Admiral Mott, who has been a good friend of mine for many years. He was Judge Advocate General of the Navy. As a former Air Force officer, I sometimes make friends with Navy people. What Bill refers to is that I was in a small group from the American Bar Association that, with the cooperation of the State Department, went to the Soviet Union around 1960. I was then active in education in Virginia. I was chairman of the school board in Richmond. With help from Ambassador Llewelyn Thompson, we had a good opportunity to do things in the Soviet Union. For example, we watched two trials, and I visited schools in Moscow, Leningrad, and Kiev, and talked to principals and some teachers, and attended one of the classes. I was impressed by the extent to which the Soviet schools identify and train specialists. They identify children at an early age who are gifted in a particular activity, physical or intellectual. They are educating specialists rather than generalists, and a major effort is made to train bright young people to be scientists. The Soviet Union may understand better than we do the importance of scientific and technological skills.

In any event, when I came back to the United States we initiated a course in the Richmond public schools on Communism and the Soviet Union. This was approved by the State Board of Education. At that time, there was no course being taught and no textbook being used in Virginia public school that focused on the Soviet Union. I trust that today our young people are being taught the facts about communism, and its ongoing threat to the freedom enjoyed only in the democracies.

**QUESTION:** The American Bar Association, as I understand it, passes on nominees for court appointments as highly qualified, qualified, and unqualified. What makes a person qualified or highly qualified? What are the criteria that the Bar Association uses in passing on the nominees?

**JUSTICE POWELL:** I suppose those categories end up being subjective to a considerable extent. The Committee of the American Bar Association, or ABA for short, has representatives in each of the fifty states. When the Justice Department submits a name, the committee initiates a thorough investigation. I pause here to say the ABA Committee dates back to the Truman administration. It has enhanced the quality of the federal judiciary that today is quite high.

I was the Virginia representative for the ABA Committee for a period of time. The Committee receives reports from the state representative, a procedure with which I was familiar. If I was not familiar with the nominee, I would have court records checked to see whether he or she had tried cases, whether the judge of the court was willing to express an opinion, and whether the individual had argued cases before the Court of Appeals. The national ABA Committee would make inquiries at the law schools.

In my case, even though I was fairly well known to the ABA, it sent a committee of three lawyers down to interview me in Richmond; I had to fill out some forms and identify cases in which I had taken part. A number of law school deans or faculty members are interviewed, particularly when the nominee is for the Supreme Court.

In the early years, the Committee made a thorough check of persons nominated for the District Court and the Court of Appeals but not for the Supreme Court. The prerogative of a president to select a nominee to sit on the Supreme Court is one of the highest prerogatives in the government of our country. For a long time the ABA Committee did not review Supreme Court nominees at all.

But it has done so at least since the Carswell nomination. In sum, I would say that in the investigations they rank one qualified, well qualified or exceptionally well qualified.

With respect to nominees for the Supreme Court, the Committee no longer uses all three categories. I believe nominees to that Court are simply ranked "not qualified" or "well qualified." I am not sure of this.

QUESTION: Justice Powell, what do you think of an age limit or a time limit, say fifteen years, for the justices to serve?

JUSTICE POWELL: Is your question whether I think there should be a retirement age for judges?

COMMENT: Yes, and also if you would limit the time they can serve.

JUSTICE POWELL: I have said publicly that if the Constitution could be amended easily—and happily it cannot be—the judges should not be allowed to sit on courts after they attain a certain age. If I had to pick an age, I would say seventy-five. Once you go on the bench, you have a very cloistered life that tends to foster longevity. A number of federal judges have stayed on the bench too long. Of course, the Constitution provides for life tenure for federal judges. There have been examples in the history of the Court when committees had to wait on Supreme Court justices who remained on the Court too long.

There is a great story about Justice Field. He served on a committee to visit Justice Miller, as I recall. Ten or fifteen years later another committee visited Justice Field. In order to start the conversation, someone asked Justice Field if he remembered when he served on a committee to visit a Justice and suggest that the time had come for that Justice to retire. Justice Field is reported to have said, "Yes, I remember that, and never a dirtier day's work have I done."

Of course, many of our greatest Justices have served well beyond age seventy-five. Oliver Wendall Holmes is the great example. On the present Court, Bill Brennan is probably in his eighty-second year and Harry Blackmun and

76

Thurgood Marshall both will be eighty this year or the next. All three of those justices are intellectually and physically fit. Thurgood has never looked physically fit. I sat beside him on the Court for the fifteen and a half years I was there. When I went up to Washington, I'd heard so many rumors about Justice Marshall's ill health that I expected to find him in fairly decrepit condition. He is overweight, and I don't think he has ever taken any exercise in his life. Thurgood says that exercise is unnecessary. Yet with the exception of one bout with pneumonia, and falling off a bicycle in Bermuda, he has missed no time from the Court since I have been there. He is intellectually keen and often very amusing.

Perhaps I should not tell this story about him, but since this is a family group, I shall. Every now and then justices whisper to each other on the bench. Thurgood leaned over to me on one occasion when a complicated securities act case was being argued, and said, "Lewis, I'll trade you my vote in this case for a future draft choice." Thurgood knows more about civil rights cases and criminal trials than anyone else on the Court, but he knew little about corporate and business law. Of course, Justice Marshall was joking with me.

Did you have a question, Mr. Thompson?

**NARRATOR:** I wondered about the kind of background you brought to the court. Social scientists are often told that they tend to get too far from the patient in the bed. Maybe legal scholars run that risk too. Your own background with the American College of Trial Lawyers, the Legal Aid Defenders, the American Bar Association, and so on, was heavily sprinkled with practical experience. Is experience important for a judge and for a justice?

**JUSTICE POWELL:** I do think it is. I think ideally one ought to have had the sort of experience that Justice Kennedy has had. He had an excellent education, he practiced law privately for a number of years, was a successful lawyer, did some teaching, and served on the 9th Circuit Court of Appeals for twelve years.

I think I was a little handicapped when I first went on the Supreme Court because, as the scholars here may know,

I believe I was the first person to go on the Supreme Court directly from the trial bar since Justice Brandeis.

Now Charles Evan Hughes went on from the practicing bar to become Chief Justice, but he had been on the Court as a justice before he resigned to run for president in 1916. I not only went directly to the Court from the practicing bar, but I also believe I practiced law longer than any other Supreme Court Justice. I don't know whether this was a handicap or not, but I was a practicing lawyer for a third of a century. My experience as a lawyer was broad. Also I had served on State and National Boards and Commissions. A justice should have had varied experience because the broader one's experience, the better equipped he or she is to deal with the complexity and variety of questions that come to the Court.

When I went on the Supreme Court, having come from a law firm where we had a number of partners and associates with expertise in various categories of law, I made a very bad proposal. I said, "Why don't we have a staff up here with a tax expert, a patent law expert, and other experts in areas in which none of us has had much experience?" Of course the answer to that is, whether we are experts or not, we have to make the judgments. If the Court relied on staff experts, they—not the Justices—would be making the judgments.

QUESTION: Justice Powell, would you care to comment on the notion that somebody who is not a lawyer could be on the Supreme Court?

JUSTICE POWELL: Someone who is not a lawyer?

QUESTION: Is it necessary to be a lawyer?

JUSTICE POWELL: The Constitution would not prohibit it, and yet I don't think there has ever been a person appointed to the United States Supreme Court or, as far as I know, to a federal court who was not a lawyer. The precedent is one that I would like to see followed. A good many of the decisions made by the Court could be made by competent scholars. That's perfectly true; but still there are numerous decisions that turn on legal and constitutional

78

questions that would be difficult for non-lawyers to decide. So I think it is desirable to adhere to the precedent of two hundred years.

I would like to make a comment here, although it is going to be a little off the subject. In thinking about where we are this evening and also about the federal judiciary, I am reminded of how two great Virginians, Jefferson and Marshall, shaped our constitutional government. They were not the warmest of friends, although they were cousins. When the Court ruled on the Nixon tapes case, one of the relevant but not directly pertinent cases that we cited was the Burr trial. It took place in Richmond, Virginia, when Marshall was Chief Justice. In those days a Supreme Court Justice didn't have too much to do, so Marshall presided first over the grand jury and then over the trial itself. He authorized the issuance of a subpoena to President Jefferson to produce certain documents that Burr wanted. There could have been a monumental crisis if Jefferson, as he was initially inclined to do, had declined to deliver the documents. Marshall then would have had to decide whether to subpoena him, and that would have raised a serious question that could have divided our young country. But Jefferson produced the documents and a crisis was avoided. The trial lasted two or three weeks and resulted in Burr's acquittal.

When the Nixon tapes case came to the Court, we were all very conscious of the fact that the United States could be facing a grave crisis. That case was argued in the middle of June, and we didn't announce the decision until 26 July. Over that period of time, with the exception of the final days in June, we had no other case to consider. All eight of us—Rehnquist stayed out of it—spent long days and nights working on that case. Each member of the Court was invited to submit memoranda to the Chief Justice who wrote the opinion. Finally we decided that presidential privilege does not extend to documents needed for a fair trial in a criminal case.

One has to wonder what would have happened if Nixon had said what President Jackson said on one occasion, "You have your decree, now enforce it." Of course, there was no way we could have enforced it. We had fifty "police" officers, but Nixon had the First Infantry Division. I think history will give Nixon high marks for accepting the judgment of the Court, although he might have been impeached. In any event, he recognized the authority of the Supreme Court of the United States to declare that even the president had to obey the law as decided by the Court.

On the other hand, we recognized that the president has a substantial privilege with respect to his duties. I'm sure the studies that have been made here at the Miller Center recognize the necessity for the confidentiality of much of what goes on in the White House. But in the course of a criminal trial, when evidence in the possession of a president is necessary for a proper defense, there was no question in the minds of any of us that the president of the United States does not have a privilege that extends that far. I repeat that I think Nixon served the country well when he accepted the judgment of the Supreme Court.

**QUESTION:** How would you rate the contribution that Chief Justice John Marshall made in strengthening the federal judiciary system?

**JUSTICE POWELL:** It was critical if you are talking about *Marbury vs. Madison,* in which Marshall made clear that the Supreme Court had the responsibility, as I mentioned at the outset, to decide what the law is. In other words, there may have been some doubt until that decision as to the degree of supremacy of the Supreme Court of the United States. Marshall was on the Court for thirty-four years and during that time I think there were sixty-odd constitutional cases decided by the Court. He wrote more than half of the opinions himself. Those were days when justices did not have law clerks, so he worked pretty hard.

It may be of interest that Chief Justice Marshall had to have a gallstone operation when he was about eighty-four years old. He went to Philadelphia and was operated on by a physician named Dr. Phillip Sing Physic, an interesting name for a surgeon. He was then one of the leading surgeons in the United States by reputation. With the assistance of a son-in-law named Randolph, he operated on Chief Justice Marshall. It is shocking to reflect that in those days there was no anaesthesia. It is reported that

80

Marshall was provided with an adequate supply of bourbon whiskey, plus a gum stick to chew on. He survived the operation and was on the Court for another three and a half years.

QUESTION: What should be the relation of a justice to public figures, journalists, and other people who are the intellectual leaders of the country? I've recently read correspondence that Justice Frankfurter had with Reinhold Niebuhr. It ranges across a broad spectrum from philosophy to current politics. Lippmann also had repeated contacts with justices. Is this a subject on which you have an opinion?

JUSTICE POWELL: On that, I have no opinion that would be very interesting beyond the fact that Frankfurter was a scholar of exceptional brilliance and carried on an elaborate correspondence long before he went on the Supreme Court. I took two classes under him when I was at the Harvard Law School and kept in touch with him. But the work of the Court was not nearly as demanding when he was there as it had become since then. Nevertheless, he was a prolific writer. Brandeis also corresponded a great deal, as did Bill Douglas. Justices now do not have time to carry on comparable correspondence. Also, it is very rare that we have an office holder, whether in the judiciary, the legislative, or the executive branch of government, as brilliant as Frankfurter. My correspondence also is largely personal, as I am not a philosopher and doubt that justices should engage in political correspondence.

Thank you very much. It has been a special privilege to have this conversation in this beautiful and historic residence.

MR. JORDAN: This completes our program. Thanks to all of you for coming and participating in our discussion, to Kenneth Thompson of the Miller Center and especially, to Justice Powell.

# V.  Judicial Selection

## JUDGE GRIFFIN BELL

NARRATOR:   Judge Bell's popularity is the best possible argument for adding an addition to the Miller Center.  This is the third time that Judge Bell has been with us: once in a discussion held jointly with the Law School on the role of the attorney general and another time for a discussion of the Carter presidency.  So actually there is very little need to introduce him; in fact, he has gained such a following here that maybe he ought to introduce me to you.  But a word may be appropriate.  Everybody, I'm sure, remembers that he was attorney general in the Carter administration from 1977-1979.  He studied at Georgia Southwestern College where he received degrees in arts and sciences at Mercer University where he took a law degree.  He practiced in Savannah and Rome following law school, and was a U.S. judge on the 5th U.S. Circuit Court of Appeals from 1961 to 1976.  He has been a partner in King and Spalding; and was chief of staff for Governor Vandiver, and close friend and associate of Jimmy Carter.  It is an honor to have Judge Bell with us again.

JUDGE BELL:   I've known President Carter since he was born, I guess.  We came from the same county.  After he received the Democratic presidential nomination, he asked me to find an attorney general, or at least he told me to start thinking about it.  Finally, somehow or another, I ended up being the attorney general.  I never found anybody to suit him.  My role as attorney general was fairly narrow because President Carter treated the Department of Justice as it should be treated, and that is nonpolitically.

He called the Department a "neutral zone" in the government. The Department of Justice has to be nonpolitical in the sense of operating on neutral principles; everyone is entitled to the same treatment. That's the way we tried to run it and we had some success at it.

One of the big things that President Carter wanted to do was change the method of selecting federal judges; he wanted to create some system where more people would apply and to expand the universe of those applying. He had put in a judicial selection system in Georgia when he was governor. It's gone well and is being copied by a number of other states. The idea was to have a commission for the federal court of appeals judges. The commission would pick out three to five people, and those names would come to the Department of Justice, and then we'd recommend to the President the best person on the list. We'd rate them from one to five. The senators were encouraged to create commissions to recommend district judges, and some did, though others did not. But I think it went well because I know that we oftentimes appointed judges who had no political connections at all. Sometimes we even appointed Republicans, though I once said on "Meet the Press" that we did not have an affirmative action program for Republicans. Most of the time the people we appointed had not really been involved in politics. They were good lawyers and had never really been active. Those kinds of people would never have been considered if we hadn't had these commissions.

I thought the commissions went well. There was a lot of confusion because people said we concentrated on finding blacks and women. Well, there were hardly any blacks or women on the federal bench and President Carter wanted to make the bench more representative of the American people. We did find a number of blacks and women, but they were always people who qualified. We brought the bench fairly well into proportion to our national population.

Incidentally, as soon as the Reagan administration came in, they did away with the commission system. They didn't like it and went back to the old way. I'm a product of the old way; I was appointed a federal judge under the old system. I was a good friend of Senators Russell and Talmadge of Georgia and also served as John Kennedy's campaign manager in Georgia. So there was hardly any way I could have missed becoming a federal judge; it had nothing to do with my ability. Probably a lot of other people were as qualified or more qualified than I was, but they hadn't had the opportunities I had. They didn't have the friends that I had. I think we need to do better than that, and that's what we were trying to do. I think we'll eventually return to a system like that instituted by President Carter because we will want to get better people for judgeships.

It is inherent in the system that one particular president will fill quite a high percentage of the federal posts. A president who stays in very long appoints about half of the federal judges because federal judges usually serve about fifteen years before they take senior status. President Carter appointed 40 percent of all the federal judges in just four years. The reason for that distortion— it's a bit high—was that we had not created any extra federal judgeships in a long, long time and about 150 new places ran up the percentage. President Reagan, in his seven years, has appointed about 50 percent of all the federal judges in the country. I read columnists who comment on this with alarm. Somehow President Reagan has managed to do a terrible thing, appointing half of the federal judges. Well, in four years, President Carter appointed 40 percent of them. Whoever is elected president next, if he stays eight years, will appoint about 50 percent again. So that is just part of the system; there is nothing wrong with it.

We liked our system. The American Bar Association rates potential judges as unqualified, qualified, well-qualified or exceptionally well-qualified. I've seen a study of the judges appointed in the administrations prior to President Carter's and in the Reagan administration, and our ratings compared very favorably with all the others. So it can't be said that our system caused inferior judges to be chosen. President Carter always appointed from the list and usually chose the number one person on the list. I remember only two occasions when he appointed the number two person. Usually he appointed whoever we thought was the best person.

That's just one of the duties of the attorney general. I spent a lot of time doing other things besides that; in fact I had Mike Egan, the associate attorney general, running that part of our operation, but I did read all the FBI files on every judge who was appointed. I had Mike read the files and also a staff person under Mike read them and then I read them because you have to be very careful; you don't want to appoint the wrong person to a job for life.

I did a lot of work in the foreign intelligence area. The attorney general has a lot to do with that. I appeared before Congress more than forty times during my tenure as attorney general. Congress interrogated me under its oversight power. We had a legislative program to run; we employed some 1,200 lawyers. These lawyers are selected through an honors program which has been in effect in the Department for about twenty-five years now, and they are some of the finest civil servants we have in the government. I've often said that if an attorney general just leaves the Justice Department lawyers alone, they will make him look good because they are good. They are the equal of the British civil service because they run the government professionally no matter which party is in power. These people are very loyal to their country and they are not that interested in politics. A lot of them take no interest in politics; they are plain professionals.

I've always opposed the special prosecutor law for this reason. I think the idea that you have to go to an outside lawyer to prosecute somebody denigrates the Department and the people in it. That law was not in effect, incidentally, when I was attorney general and we were able to prosecute Bert Lance. Nobody thought that we weren't doing our job. We even investigated President Carter once; I appointed a special lawyer from New York to investigate the case. He was a Republican, incidentally, who had been a U.S. attorney in New York, but at the time was just a practicing lawyer. He investigated the Carter peanut warehouse because there had been a lot of stories that Carter had laundered money through the warehouse to finance his campaign. This was not true, as the investigation showed. I tell this story just to show that without the benefit of all these special prosecutors, we were able to do our duty, even if it involved the President. That's the kind of place the Department of Justice is.

President Carter was very supportive of the Department, and he had a high regard for the rule of law. He wanted the Department to be as neutral as possible. He exempted me from all political activities; I never had to go to any kind of political meeting while I was attorney general. He didn't think that it was right for the attorney general to be going to political meetings. That's quite a change because when Roosevelt was President, the man who nominated him for a second term was Homer Cummings, the attorney general. He went to the convention and nominated Mr. Roosevelt. That wouldn't happen today, I don't think, in either party. Certainly it would not have happened under President Carter.

I also have some strong views on the National Security Council, whose meetings I often attended. We sometimes discussed covert operations, but I was not invited to all the meetings. Since I've left the government, I've often wondered what the system was, and why I would be invited sometimes and not other times. I think we would have been spared a lot of trouble in recent days if the attorney general had been required to go to National Security Council meetings at which covert operations were discussed. It would be very hard for anything illegal to be done if the attorney general were there and had to give his or her views. That would be one thing I would do to improve the system.

I found out this morning that Clark Clifford has recently come out to say the same thing. I've never discussed it with him, but it seems like an obvious safeguard. The President is not at those meetings, and he has to depend on the people who are. If something were going to be done that was illegal, I can't imagine an attorney general who wouldn't stop it, or if you didn't stop it, at least go in and tell the President. I don't believe there has been a President since Watergate, maybe before that, who wouldn't stop something illegal. Today the President has to be at pains not to do anything illegal. I think that is enough. I'll take some questions.

**QUESTION:** Is the scope of the work of the Department too broad? You have, on the one hand, the FBI and on the other hand you are selecting judges. Now wouldn't it be better if you concentrated more on the straight legal aspect of the work rather than on peripheral activities?

**JUDGE BELL:** That's a very good question. Personally, I would remove the Immigration Service from the Department of Justice. The Immigration Service has been in several departments; nobody really wants it. It finally was placed in the Department of Justice during World War II. It had been in the State Department and in the Labor Department. It is a vast agency with a lot of problems. It probably doesn't get enough attention—at least I didn't give it enough attention as attorney general. There were so many other things that had to be done with the FBI and the DEA (Drug Enforcement Administration) besides operating divisions of the Department itself: the Office of Legal Counsel, the Solicitor General's office, the Civil Division, the Criminal Division, the Tax Division, and so on. So there probably is more there than can reasonably be handled.

For generations we have argued whether the attorney general should have anything to do with the selection of federal judges, the argument being that the attorney general has more cases in court than anyone else, therefore he ought not pick the judges. In my experience, however, I haven't seen any judges leaning over backwards to help the attorney general. I used to be a judge myself, so I speak from experience. Moreover, I don't know where else we would put the selection of judges. If it were in the White House, I would fear for the nation. But somebody has to try to be as objective as possible. A lot of times the White House owes a political favor. You have to understand that the White House is the center of the politics of the nation and these judges ought to be at least screened by somebody else. I can't think of a better place than the Department.

But I'd start out by spinning off the Immigration Service and sending it somewhere else (though nobody else would want it). It is a problem. That is a very difficult area of government to operate.

**QUESTION:** What importance would you attach to trial experience in the appointment of federal judges? I'll divide that into two parts: district judges and court of appeals judges. Quite recently a professor at the University of Virginia was nominated for the court of appeals, and there was a big hullabaloo because he'd never tried a case. However, he was confirmed. I don't know him, but I assume that he is a very, very capable lawyer and is qualified to handle any case that might come before the court.

**JUDGE BELL:** I think you'd need trial experience if you were going to be a district judge. I don't think trial experience is at all necessary to be a court of appeals judge or a supreme court justice. I'm sure Justice Rutledge and Justice Frankfurter never tried a case, and both were good justices. This young man you were talking about is Jay Wilkinson, and I've read some of his opinions. He seems to be doing a good job. You wouldn't want to have everyone on the court of appeals with the same qualifications; I think it is a good thing to have some diversity. When I was on the 5th Circuit Court of Appeals, it was the largest court in the country. We handled Texas right through Florida, and all the civil rights cases of those days. We always enjoyed having two or three district judges who had been elevated to the court of appeals, and they knew a good deal more than the rest of us. I was a trial lawyer, but I was never a trial judge. I thought the mix was good, and I think to have a professor, someone who is really learned in the law, on the court of appeals is a good thing. It brings a flavor of scholarship that you might not otherwise get from some rundown lawyers like myself.

**QUESTION:** Judge Bell, do you have any comments about the selection of Judge Bork as a nominee for the Supreme Court? How do you feel about that? Do you think we've done him an injustice?

**JUDGE BELL:** I'm too biased to answer that question. I testified in favor of Judge Bork, and I thought the whole exercise was anti-intellectual. The process was converted into a plebiscite. Whether you were for or against Bork, you have to recognize that that isn't a good thing for the future. Are we going to do that every time there is a controversy about somebody? Are we going to start running polls to see whether the American people like the nominee? That isn't the way the system is supposed to work. That was what I thought happened in the Bork case. The very day I testified I read a *New York Times*-ABC poll and I told the Senate Committee that I could see what was happening, that they were going to start asking the American people if they wanted so and so to be on the Supreme Court. The public wouldn't know how to select a justice but they would give their opinion and the Senate would follow. Of course all the senators said, "Oh, we wouldn't do that, no, no." But Bork didn't last long after that.

**QUESTION:** Judge Bell, former Chief Justice Warren Burger has, on a number of occasions, suggested that the Supreme Court's work load is too great. He seems to have recommended a screening committee between the appellate division and the Supreme Court. Do you think that would be possible or could work?

**JUDGE BELL:** I think it could work, but I've never favored it. I think the Supreme Court justices ought to work more and use more discipline about what they do with their time. Cutting down from four law clerks would be a step in the right direction because they've got to deal with all these law clerks, argue with them about everything. I finally got up to three law clerks and I left. I spent all my time working with the law clerks, or rather working *for* them. In the old days the Supreme Court handled just as many cases as they do now and they had one law clerk, and then they got up to two, then three, now they've got four. I think they need to exercise more discipline in which cases they take.

I don't think the situation is quite as bad as Justice Burger contends, but if we wanted to go to that system it could be made to work. What you'd do is call in court of appeals judges on special assignment for three to six months to do the screening. But you see the law clerks screen at the Court now. The way the Court works now you can't even get a petition placed on the conference calendar unless one justice moves to put it on the calendar. So the vast number of over five thousand cases are never even considered in a conference. So I think they are working it out. Not all of the present Supreme Court Justices favor a screening committee. I believe Chief Justice Rehnquist favors it; I don't know about the others. I think that they probably ought to go along like they are for a while.

**NARRATOR:** Every president, upon entering office, talks about reinstating cabinet government and every time it fizzles out after a while. A lot of power has gravitated to the White House. Do you have any recommendations or thoughts about that?

**JUDGE BELL:** It is almost impossible to have cabinet government today because a large number of the Cabinet officers are no more than bureau heads. They really are not doing the same thing as the secretary of state, the secretary of defense, the secretary of the treasury, and the attorney general. The Labor Department is looking after labor interests; Commerce is looking after business problems; Housing is looking after housing interests. I don't think they have any responsibility for the broad problems of the nation. I attended many Cabinet meetings where President Carter would go around the table and ask people to report on what they were doing and it was really a mish-mash when we heard from those type of Cabinet officers. President Carter finally abandoned the idea of these meetings where everyone reported, though it took him about a year and a half before he did it.

President Reagan is doing something a little different. He has Cabinet committees to which he assigns things which fall to two or three different Cabinet officers. He puts them together on a committee. You could go back, I think, to the old system that George Washington and some of the earlier presidents used where four or five Cabinet officers served as an executive committee. If I were president, I think I would try that, and we'd discuss broad governmental problems, particularly anything that might relate to several departments at the same time. Then I'd try to remove these agency-type Cabinet officers from the Cabinet, though I admit that would be almost impossible to do. Congress wants to add more Cabinet posts. They're going to give the Veteran's Administration a Cabinet post. I guess we could just deemphasize these agencies, but right now you couldn't have cabinet government. It would be impossible because it would be terrible government. I'd hate to think what it would be like if everybody in the Cabinet could vote on all these things. Lincoln used to get a vote from his Cabinet officers, you know. But he said, "There are ten votes; nine nays and my aye; the ayes have it." That's my system.

QUESTION: Mr. Bell, one of the things that concerns some of us is this business of appointment for life. Do you think that we can go on with appointments for life?

JUDGE BELL: Well, I've testified in Congress several times that we ought to amend the Constitution to have a fifteen year term for a judge, and then if he wanted to serve another term, he would have to stand for reappointment. That would eliminate people who really weren't in shape to keep serving. I haven't found any great wave of enthusiasm for this. In fact, I've never heard anybody favor this except me.

COMMENT: Maybe after Claude Pepper leaves you will be able to testify.

JUDGE BELL: It is very difficult to amend the Constitution, as you know, but I think in the years ahead we may come to something like this. I think if you've given fifteen years of service as a judge, you've rendered about all the service you need to render. We've gotten to the point now where we can't get anybody off the Supreme Court. You asked the question of whether they are overworked. Well, I don't know, but they stay there. We've got one justice now who is eighty-one, and three or four are over seventy-five; if they were overworked, I would think they would give some thought to leaving.

When I was a court of appeals judge, we had a district judge in Texas who had been appointed by Roosevelt. He was holding court when he was well into his nineties. His staff would pick him up and put him on the bench. So we sent somebody to talk with him about retiring and he said

92

he couldn't retire. He said "President Roosevelt appointed me for life; I'm still living." He was Judge Davidson in Fort Worth, if you want to know who he was; he had been the lieutenant governor of Texas.

QUESTION: Judge Bell, if the Supreme Court rules that the appointment of special investigators is unconstitutional, would you care to predict what the future will be in the way of investigations of people thought to have been in violation of the law?

JUDGE BELL: Well, I don't know how the Supreme Court is going to rule. I don't favor the Special Prosecutor Law myself, but most of all I don't favor Congress cutting constitutional corners. If there is some doubt about the constitutionality of a special prosecutor, then why have doubt? Why not do it the way it could be done, legally and constitutionally? That would be to have the president appoint a number of special counselors, have a panel. They could serve on into the next administration. These people would all be confirmed by the Senate, then it would be legal. That's what the Constitution says. Why Congress rejects this is beyond me. Then we'd have a prosecutor who has been confirmed by the Senate.

The second thing about the Special Prosecutor Law that I object to is that the public doesn't know what the charter is. Judges sign orders and tell the prosecutors what they are supposed to do; we don't know what that is. Right now there are two secret special prosecutors. Can you imagine secret prosecutors in a free country? This kind of thing won't do and we'll finally have to come to our senses. But I would think that even if the law is held unconstitutional, we will have special prosecutors. The American people have been told that they can't trust the Department of Justice to prosecute everybody, that we've got to have these special prosecutors. So I think we will have a panel of them. They will be nominated just like a U.S. attorney or an attorney general and confirmed by the Senate. At least then we know who they are, that they've been investigated by the FBI, that they've paid their taxes, and so on. They will be treated as other prosecutors or judges. Then we will have more confidence in them; at

93

least I would. I don't like the system we have now; I think it is anti-democratic. It is an overreaction.

Right now the Justice Department is having a lot of trouble. If we had a popular attorney general, people would probably be paying more attention to what I am saying. Right now people cry that the attorney general is under investigation. Well, he might be, but that doesn't mean the system can't work. If it is something he's had a dealing with, he can't handle it anyway; it has to go down the line until you find somebody who is qualified to handle it. In the Bert Lance case I disqualified myself, and it was passed down until it got to some career people and they handled the whole thing; they indicted, prosecuted, and tried him. That's the way the system works. People will be prosecuted; you don't have to worry. The problem in this country, it seems to me, is that we prosecute too many people. Not many people are getting off.

QUESTION: Judge Bell, do you think there is more and more difficulty in keeping a separation of powers in the government? It seems that recently there has been more infringement of the rights of the executive branch by the legislative branch.

JUDGE BELL: Oh, yes. This has gotten to be quite a problem, particularly in foreign policy. We are seeing something in Nicaragua, with the Speaker of the House intervening directly there, that I didn't think I'd ever see. And people are not outraged about it. It was quite a surprise to me, but the columnists are not writing much about it. It is in direct conflict with the Constitution and with the system that has evolved, and it makes it impossible for the President to fashion and execute foreign policy. And in our system the president is responsible for doing it, right or wrong. But now we've got two groups running foreign policy: we've got the President and we've got the House. The Senate hasn't been in on it yet; if they get in it, we'll have three groups.

QUESTION: Would the Supreme Court or court system have any recourse at all?

**JUDGE BELL:** No, the court wouldn't handle it because it is a political question. A lot of these questions are political. The legality of the Vietnam War was taken to the Supreme Court several times, but they never would handle it on the grounds that it was a political question. I had to defend the President in a suit brought by Senator Goldwater when we abrogated the treaty with Taiwan after we recognized the People's Republic of China. We won that case on the grounds that it was a political question.

There are a number of suits pending now by members of Congress who are trying to get things done that President Reagan won't agree to, and they will all be thrown out as political questions. So we just have to leave some things to the voters. Maybe in the long run it will straighten out, but it is a worrisome thing to me right now.

**QUESTION:** Judge Bell, from what you've said, I gather that you believe a lot depends on the president as to whether the attorney general's office functions neutrally or more politically. I agree with that. You also indicate that Supreme Court justices might do better if fewer law clerks were available because law clerks have more administrative than legal experience.

**JUDGE BELL:** I'm sorry I said that because I'm never going to win another case in the Supreme Court. [Laughter]

**QUESTION:** I have a feeling you have some more reforms up your sleeve. Would you, for example, be for institutionalizing the commission system of nomination? What other reforms have you in mind?

**JUDGE BELL:** That would be one thing I'd do with these commissions. I would do that. I would depoliticize the selection of judges. I would prohibit the Justice Department from asking people questions about their philosophy. I think that is an abomination. We never asked anybody about their philosophy when I was attorney general. It is absolutely improper, in my judgment, to do that.

The other thing that I think would improve the Department of Justice—that's all I really know much about—would be to eliminate senators' patronage which

95

allows them to appoint U.S. attorneys. Let the attorney general pick the U.S. attorneys subject to presidential approval, which you always have to get, and Senate confirmation.

I've already mentioned the other reform. I would have the attorney general attend all meetings of the National Security Council. If he couldn't make it, he would send his deputy. The secretary of defense attends or sends a deputy; the secretary of state attends or sends a deputy. They are always there, but not the attorney general. So there are a number of little things like that, none of them drastic, and all which could be done by a president. But the problem is that the next president may change the system.

I have a feeling that maybe the presidents don't understand enough about the government. We elect presidents who perhaps haven't studied the system enough.

**COMMENT:** Sometimes candidates run against it.

**JUDGE BELL:** I received a letter from Governor Dukakis asking me to support him. He sent a copy of one of his speeches. I read the speech and in it he called on every American to write a letter to Speaker Wright to thank him for what he had done to help the situation in Nicaragua. You see he needs to know more about the system and the allocation of power under the Constitution. Maybe he thought that was a good thing, but he wasn't thinking about making the system work correctly.

**QUESTION:** More than one government agency is involved in the war on drugs. Would you care to comment on the attorney general's role in the current war on drugs?

**JUDGE BELL:** The attorney general ought to be the leader in the government because the FBI and the Drug Enforcement Administration are under the attorney general. Traditionally the FBI has done very little work on drugs. Director Hoover didn't want the FBI working on the drug problem because he said it might corrupt some of the agents. Of course when he lived we didn't have a drug problem; we have one terrible drug problem now. You have to use the Coast Guard. You have to get some help from the military; that is, the *rest* of the military if you consider the Coast Guard military. And that was slow in coming. We can track airplanes and ships, but somehow or another we are not interdicting as much as we should be. A lot is going to have to be done in other countries to dry up the sources. We had good luck with Mexico when I was attorney general because their national policy was very much opposed to marijuana. They thought it had a bad effect on their people, so they destroyed the poppy fields. Cocaine had not come onto the scene yet. The Mexicans were very cooperative.

But I believe in the end the only way we are going to do anything about the drug problem is to mount some sort of a national campaign against drug use. If we don't stop the use of drugs, it's hard to keep people out of the market. Apparently we are the largest drug market in the world. There is a lot of money to be made. We prosecute these pilots, some former military pilots, who get $25,000 cash up front for one flight to Columbia and $25,000 to return. That's tax-free money. Or he can even pay taxes on it and still be pretty well off. That's the kind of money for the little people—think what the people who run it make. So we have to do more about the users, dry up the market, and that would be something the president would have to do.

**QUESTION:** How would you do that? Arrest them?

**JUDGE BELL:** Use the office of the president as a "bully pulpit"; get the people fired up on it, get it organized. There's hardly anything that we shouldn't do to stop it, but we are not getting it stopped now.

The drug problem is a terrible problem. I was talking to a client recently who has a mill about fifty miles from Atlanta. He said they'd always tried to employ 70 percent white employees and 30 percent black employees because that is the kind of population they had in this little rural county. He said they couldn't hire white people because they were failing the drug test. The blacks weren't failing so their numbers were creeping up, and they were getting out of balance, which wasn't a bad thing. I mean there was no reason to get excited, but he was appalled at the number

97

of people who wanted a job, but who couldn't pass a drug test. That's in one little town. I've talked to people who run corporations and they say this is happening all over the country. They don't test people on the job, only people applying for a job. There is no telling how many people they'd have to fire if they started testing on the job. So this is a massive problem. It hasn't been talked about enough.

Probably in this little Georgia mill town—it is a beautiful town—people would be outraged if somebody talked about the drugs in their community. But that's what the drug tests show.

**QUESTION:** The problem you have there is that if you try to let someone go who has a drug or alcohol problem, the government says you can't fire them because they are sick. What do you do about that?

**JUDGE BELL:** These tests I'm talking about are for people who are trying to get a job. So if they test positive, you don't have to give them a job. I think there is a case in the Supreme Court right now concerning the testing of public employees. A district judge ruled that public employees couldn't be tested and the appellate court reversed that and I think it may be in the Supreme Court now. I don't know who the public employees were, whether they were air controllers or some other public employees. We will be seeing more and more of this in the future though; this will become a big battle. It would be unfortunate if we had to test everybody everyday, but if you have some reason to think people are using drugs on the job, it seems to me you could develop some sort of reasonable sampling system. I don't know how that would work out. We'll just have to wait and see what the Supreme Court does with this.

**QUESTION:** Judge Bell, when there is a new administration, how is the transition process managed as far as the departments are concerned?

**JUDGE BELL:** I'm not familiar with any transition process except the one we used in the Carter administration. We had a young man in our law firm, Jack Watson, who was asked by President Carter, after he had the nomination, to set up a transition team. He assembled ten or twelve staff people, mostly lawyers, to find out what jobs needed to be filled and to get together lists of people. I thought they did a good job. In fact, I used some of their lists when I was looking for people for the Department of Justice. I would imagine that all of the candidates do about the same thing. There are a lot of people who would like to come into the government. You can't get as many good people as you would like, but we are a very patriotic country, and if you ask people to come into the government—particularly if the president asks them—they find it hard to refuse, though it is more difficult now because of all these disclosure rules. A lot of people don't want to disclose that they have a lot of money or that they don't have any money. It works both ways. And a lot of people resent the fact that you are invading their privacy by asking all these things.

I had made up my mind that I would never go back into the government when I left the attorney general's office after going through two weeks of Senate hearings. I didn't ever want to go through that again. But President Carter called and asked me to go to Madrid to head the American delegation to the Helsinki Accord, a follow-up meeting, and I agreed to do it. I received a set of forms to fill out from the Senate Foreign Relations Committee, from the White House, and from somebody else. I had three sets of forms to fill out. I sent them all back and called President Carter and told him I couldn't do it because I just wasn't going to fill out all these forms again, have a hearing, be embarrassed, and so on. So he called Warren Christopher (Vance was out of the country), and told him to figure out a way to get me appointed as a special ambassador without having to fill out any forms. So I was appointed a special ambassador for six months. I didn't fill out one form. So it worked out all right.

**NARRATOR:** May I ask a follow-up to Mrs. Cromwell's question? We had a commission, as you may know, looking at presidential transitions. It has a report forthcoming, and Senator Glenn's Government Operations Committee has looked at transitions and there have been some other groups. Their recommendations go in one direction, our recommendations go the other way. They want to increase the budget for the transition group from two to three million; we want to cut the money because of the hairdressers and tuxedos and all of these things have been paid for recently with the transition fund. Do you have any thoughts about the size of the transition operation? I don't think yours was one of the larger ones.

**JUDGE BELL:** Basically I don't think you ought to throw money at every problem. When Jack Watson started working on the transition, we didn't have any money. In fact, until now, I hadn't realized that we ever received money from the government for our transition. It isn't that hard to handle transitions. First you need the list of all the jobs you are going to fill. If you fill the top two or three layers of jobs, then those appointees can fill out the other jobs. I found people for the Justice Department that the transition group never heard of. I knew where good people were. I think we need a good transition, but I can't imagine increasing the money. Two million dollars ought to be more than adequate. That's a lot of money just to do a personnel operation.

**NARRATOR:** We all look forward to a continued relationship with you. Thank you so much.

**JUDGE BELL:** Thank you.

# VI. Personnel Policy and
# the Bureau of the Budget

## EDGAR B. YOUNG

NARRATOR: An area touched from time to time but never really dealt with in the manner which some of us might wish, is personnel selection, management, and the administration of government. You will recall that when Sam Nunn was here he spoke of arms control as being an arcane and abstract subject. Despite the efforts of Frederick Mosher, Ed Young, Paul David, and others who have written on this topic, some see public administration as having these same characteristics. The most difficult presentations I had to make at the Rockefeller Foundation dealt with public administration. The response to proposals which I thought were exactly right was always, "You can't teach administration and you can't really study it either. It is too individualistic and depends on the person." This notion remains ingrained in the minds of many Americans.

On the other hand, public administration seems central to every other topic one touches. Thomas Corcoran, when he spoke here, made the comment that the success of any administration was determined by what he called "the first thousand men down," or the appointees chosen to fill the one thousand top positions.

Frederick Mosher, two younger colleagues, and I were part of a group that addressed the problem of presidential transition. I don't think our report did the subject full justice as far as the administration and personnel aspects of the transition were concerned, but those three published a very significant book on the subject.

# PERSONNEL POLICY AND THE BUREAU OF THE BUDGET

Several participants in our transition study group, the former chairman of NBC, and an executive vice president of IBM, for example, talked about the personnel selection methods of the large corporations. We called on Cliff Garvin of the Exxon Corporation, and he lectured us on the differences between personnel selection in the private sector and the much more hasty and sometimes ill-considered selection process of the federal government, which must be done between election day and inauguration day. The report addresses this subject, but it surely doesn't exhaust it. In the Commission Report on Presidential Transitions we dealt more with the problems than with the answers.

Another contribution for which the Miller Center can take modest credit, and for which the author can take all the credit, is Frederick Mosher's book, *A Tale of Two Agencies: A Comparative Analysis of the General Accounting Office and the Office of Management and Budget.* He has also written on today's subject, the Bureau of the Budget, in its earlier period. Donald Kettl, a young public administration scholar at the University of Virginia, has also published a book under Miller Center auspices, entitled *The Regulation of American Federalism.* These efforts, though substantial, surely are the beginning rather than the end of inquiry.

In terms of Miller Center interests, it is entirely appropriate that we have some discussion on the subject of personnel policy, especially in light of the fiftieth anniversary of the Brownlow Report. Frederick Mosher helped organize a colloquium commemorating the Report. We have a little book on our bookshelves that resulted from that effort. It contains papers by James Fesler and others, and a long commentary by Luther Gulick, which suggests that whenever one addresses the problems of government, personnel selection is central.

Ed Young is a long-time friend. He was born in Anderson, Indiana; he received both his bachelor's and his L.L.D. from DePauw University; he did postgraduate work at American University, at the London School of Economics, and at the University of Pennsylvania. In a sense, he has had two careers. In the 1930s he served as assistant to the director of the U.S. Employment Service; director of personnel in the Bureau of the Budget from 1939 to 1945;

assistant to the executive director of the New York Port Authority; and a consultant on overseas personnel. That's the public sector career of Ed Young.

In the private sector Ed Young follows Lindsay Kimball, Raymond Fosdick, and others who played the role of principal adviser to John D. Rockefeller, III. The area in which I came to have the greatest respect for him, though, was in the conception and building of the Lincoln Center for the Performing Arts. If you don't think that was difficult to bring about, let me tell you it was like pulling teeth to get even a small amount of money from the Rockefeller Foundation. It was said that if John D. Rockefeller III wanted to build Lincoln Center, he ought to pay for it. Ed Young had to contend with that. The other problem was that all the other foundations felt they had their own programs. I well remember one junior colleague saying to the president of the Rockefeller Foundation and myself, after having expressed great skepticism about Lincoln Center, "I can let you have $30,000." The prevalence of that kind of attitude called for consummate diplomacy, tireless consensus building, and the generation of enthusiasm.

Ed Young, first as secretary, then as acting president, then as executive vice president of Lincoln Center, and finally as chairman of the Building Committee, accomplished just that. So I feel that we are in the mainstream of Miller Center interests in turning to somebody with a lifetime of experience in this area. Ed will talk with us and then answer questions about certain issues of personnel selection and administration.

MR. YOUNG: Thank you, Ken. Your reference to my dual career prompts me to tell an anecdote related to Lincoln Center. Some of you may recall that there was a very brief period when General Maxwell Taylor was the president of Lincoln Center. The Cuban missile crisis intervened and terminated what might have been, for him and for Lincoln Center, a very fruitful period of executive leadership. In that brief period I came to know and greatly admire General Taylor. Late one afternoon, while discussing a variety of things that needed to be done for Lincoln Center, the

103

General turned to me and said, "Ed, nothing in the Pentagon was ever so complicated."

Let me say, first of all, that since I did leave the federal government more than forty years ago, I have tried to keep modestly abreast of what is happening in governmental affairs and governmental administration. And for that reason I've appreciated being kept on the mailing list of the Miller Center. When your bulletin came out some time ago indicating that you had honored the Brownlow Committee, I was moved to write my old friend, Ken, and thank the Miller Center for honoring what I have always regarded as one of the really significant advances in the art of public and governmental administration. It brought to my mind and to Ken's the role I had in one aspect of the implementation of the Brownlow Committee recommendations, namely, the improvement and advancement of personnel management largely within the civil service. Though I wasn't involved on the level of presidential appointees, I hope that what little I have to say to you today might serve as a footnote to your observance of the Brownlow Committee anniversary and its recommendations, all of which were directed toward implementing the role of the president as the executive manager of the federal government.

Some of you will recall that the Committee regarded the Bureau of the Budget (BOB), which was then in the Treasury Department, as the nucleus of the management arm of the president. On the Committee's recommendations, the BOB was moved by executive order from the Treasury Department into the newly created executive office of the president in 1939. Particular recommendations of the Brownlow Report pertained to the six administrative assistants to the president, who were to be men with a "passion for anonymity." That has a particularly nostalgic ring when one thinks of the present day and the numerous assistants and assistants to assistants to the president in the White House. The Bureau of the Budget had been a very limited fiscal agency within the Treasury Department. In its new position, the BOB brought the National Resources Planning Board in as a closely associated agency; the Central Statistical Board came in and functioned very much as a reviewer of the whole information gathering process of the government.

A new division in the new Bureau of the Budget was the Division of Administrative Management, headed by Donald Stone. His name may be quite familiar to some of you, as Don was one of the university deans of public administration. It was Don with whom I worked most closely. At the top of the hierarchy was Harold Smith, the former budget officer for the State of Michigan, who had been appointed by President Roosevelt as the director of the newly created BOB. I was borrowed from the United States Employment Service to do a short-term job, chiefly to aid Donald Stone in the initial expansion of the Bureau. No more than twenty or thirty employees came over from the Treasury Department. The new role of the BOB involved a rather massive personnel expansion, and it was all to be done under civil service. I had had some reputation in public administration circles for having initiated and administered the so-called "merit system" in the United States Employment Service. I had developed a process of examination and selection of personnel in the State Employment Services during the depths of the Depression, very early on in the Roosevelt administration.

One of the innovative practices in our Employment Service merit system was the introduction of oral interviews. These were designed to achieve some measure of the personality traits and human relations traits that were deemed essential for those kinds of positions. I think that was one of the reasons that Don Stone was motivated to seek my services. He had already negotiated with the Civil Service Commission that the Bureau would aid the Commission in the preparation of the examinations and in the process of recruiting a whole cadre of new administrative personnel. Intent on implementing the recommendations of the Brownlow Committee, the Civil Service Commission sought to improve the management staffs of all agencies throughout the government. So I was brought into the Bureau and worked very closely, for a period of three or four months, with the people in the Civil Service Commission. We invented a new title for certain positions: "administrative analyst." These positions had to be filled in the various classification levels, from the

105

highest down to the entry level. We then developed written examination materials, including short-answer questions and essay questions, as well as a system of personal interviews for the recruitment of the higher grade positions. The Commission established registers that were very widely used for the next three or four years. Our recruiting process attracted a fair amount of attention in academic circles and particularly in those institutions that had schools of public administration. It also proved to be a valuable recruiting mechanism to bring in people at higher than entry level positions, that is for lateral entry.

After a few months I was asked to transfer to the Bureau of the Budget and I became its personnel director. Allow me to digress for just a moment and remind you that in the late 1930s the whole concept of personnel management in the federal government was, by any standard, very rudimentary. In most of the departments and agencies, with the notable exception of the Department of Agriculture, personnel work was the responsibility of the departmental chief clerk. There were no personnel officers, or personnel directors in the departments and agencies until the 1930s. And the Civil Service Commission, which of course had been established as a reform measure, was characterized by an obsession with its control and regulatory functions.

The concept of personnel management being a service and an aid to the line management of an agency appeared to be a rather new concept in the 1930s. I think that this concept is so well accepted today that it is hard to realize how rudimentary it was in the 1930s.

My role in the Bureau evolved from being the personnel officer to becoming the representative of its director on matters of government-wide personnel policy and development. In that role some very interesting relationships developed.

Bill McReynolds, [who is the same Bill McReynolds who later headed the Office of Emergency Management] was the first of the six presidential administrative assistants, and was designated "liaison officer for personnel management" in the newly formed executive office. McReynolds was a wise old man. Even before I came on the scene, he had decided that instead of building up a staff to carry out his function,

106

he would utilize the staff of the Bureau of the Budget to do so. This had been an agreement he had worked out with Don Stone.

Bill McReynolds' office on the second floor of the old Executive Office Building was about four doors down the hall from mine, and we had a most rewarding, satisfactory, and rather informal relationship. He would pop into my office or I would pop into his. As things gradually evolved, I transmitted items that required the President's knowledge, concurrence, or signature, though it was McReynolds, of course, who had access to the President. In all of my time in the Bureau I never personally conferred with President Roosevelt. It was always done either through Harold Smith or through Bill McReynolds. These were simple yet enormously successful modes of operation, and they were not cluttered by great staffs and extensive processes of review.

What did this function of representing the director of the budget in personnel management mean and how was it conducted? Let me address the latter question first. I've already mentioned the relationship with McReynolds. A second set of relationships evolved with the commissioners and the senior staff of the Civil Service Commission. The building of the Budget Bureau began in 1939. It was only shortly thereafter that we were deep into the war preparation program and, of course, we continued with this during the war period after Pearl Harbor. With the expansion of the federal government occurring parallel to the war preparations, it became clear that the Civil Service Commission was really quite ill prepared. I think it is fair to say that the Commission itself was not able to take any constructive initiatives in the field of personnel management until Arthur Fleming was appointed its commissioner. Arthur had energy and administrative skills far beyond those of any existing Commission members. By subtle direction of the President, he was permitted to function as the executive officer of the Civil Service Commission. Arthur and I had a very close relationship, and when things needed to be done that involved the Commission, we could work them out. I had very effective relationships with the senior staff people in their hierarchy, that is, the examining division which was their recruiting mechanism, and particularly their classification division. I worked very closely with them on classification matters and on the consideration of the Commission's promotion regulations which became a very vital matter for improving morale within the service as it was rapidly expanding.

A third mode of operation was obtained within the Bureau as the Division of Administrative Management began to study organization and management in one after another department and agency and to create a pattern of organization for each of the newly established war agencies. Most of the war agencies had officially come into existence by executive order, all of which were drafted in the Bureau's Division of Administrative Management. My relationship with their staff consisted of consultation and assistance in drafting the provisions of those executive orders which would deal with personnel matters in these newly established agencies.

Still another set of external relationships that dealt with government-wide personnel matters evolved with the Council on Personnel Administration. I don't know whether or not this organization continues to exist in the federal government, but in the early 1940s it was an enormously useful mechanism. It was composed of the personnel directors of all departments and agencies, many of whom were new to their jobs or new to the federal government. The Council was chaired by a very wise ex-congressman from New York, Frederick Davenport, who had recruited several extremely able staff people, such as Henry Reining. I think at one time James Mitchell, who later became Civil Service Commissioner, might have been on Davenport's staff.

The Council on Personnel Administration in those days met bi-monthly. My role was to aid the chairman of the Council and his staff in developing an agenda for these bi-monthly meetings, and to bring up those topics that most urgently needed the exchange of information between the various directors of personnel. Some agency directors were much further advanced than others and we used these meetings to get reports from those who had successful programs. In retrospect, a great number of the more constructive concepts concerning the role of personnel officers and their staffs, and their relationship to managerial officials and executives in the departments and agencies, seem to have emerged from these Council of Personnel Administration discussions.

I also found myself heavily involved in the BOB's relations with Congress. In this early experimental period of organizing the administration we rather frequently encountered matters requiring legislation. As the spokesman for the director of the BOB, I had the good fortune of developing a mutually helpful relationship with the chairmen of the House and the Senate Civil Service Committees. Chairman Ramspeck of the House Committee, who later became the chairman of the Civil Service Commission, was a very intelligent and dedicated member of Congress. He, his staff, and I had one of those fortunate working relationships. When he wanted to know how the administration would react to certain matters proposed in Congress, I could help him get the answers. Conversely, when the BOB needed to know something about legislative matters—and in that period salary and pay matters frequently involved legislation—he could help me. My role for the BOB was, in effect, an extension of the role of the director of the budget for clearing all pending legislation, and advising the heads of departments and agencies on what was and was not in accord with the president's program. If I went down to the Hill, I would indicate what the President's program was and what the reasons were behind the particular legislation we sought.

And, finally, I found myself in the curious role of continuing a relationship with those in the press who were interested in these kinds of matters. Those of you who know anything about Washington in the late 1930s and the wartime years will recall that there was a daily column in the *Washington Post* by Jerry Klutz on matters of federal personnel administration. Jerry Klutz was the public purveyor of information on behalf of the civil service employees. Once more I had the good fortune of being able to develop a very helpful working relationship with Klutz. I found he could be trusted, and he found that he could trust information that I gave him. He would observe my requests for confidentiality and this made our relationship work. When one thinks of today's era of investigative journalism, it is very hard to imagine that such a relationship could have existed, but in fact it did.

Let me now turn to the matter of salary and pay legislation. The Congress then, as now, tried to maintain a very rigid control over the salary levels in the federal government. As we came into the war period, a very dramatic difference had emerged between the wage and salary policies for the civil service positions and the so-called Wage Board's positions in the navy yards' arsenals, and so on. The latter recognized the need for comparability with prevailing wage rates in the localities where people were employed. On the other hand, the Civil Service Classification System was very rigid, and had a very limited number of grades and little or no relationship to the prevailing compensation rates in parallel private positions.

We never broke out of that rigid system. But we did, by legislation, succeed in increasing the number of grades, particularly in the higher administrative echelons where there were the widest pay differentials between the government and the private sector. I don't think we solved that problem completely, and I don't think it has been solved today, or at least not to any great satisfaction. This is an inherent problem of the relationship with the Congress.

I think we made considerable progress in personnel management by thinking of it as a service aid to line officers for accomplishing their job. The effectiveness of this arrangement differed with departments and agencies, depending upon the quality of leadership of the secretary or the assistant secretaries and the quality of leadership of the personnel directors. It was an era in which there was some progress.

If I tried to examine what the keys were to whatever success we did have—and I claim only modest successes—I think foremost was the atmosphere of professionalism that characterized that initial period in the Bureau of the Budget. From the director down through Donald Stone and the others, the attitude prevailed that we were in the executive office to serve the president, whoever he might be. We were there to work in a professional, not an ideological or political manner. And I think this professional spirit pervaded the entire Bureau. I could name a number of people who went on to very high administrative positions in the federal government that had gone through this period in the BOB in which devoted public service attitudes prevailed.

The second key to success in the field of governmental personnel administration was our continuous emphasis and our gradual achievement of the concept of personnel management as a service rather than as a control function.

And third, I think we were able to accomplish whatever we accomplished by maintaining a variety of relationships with people in other departments, in Congress, and other institutions. The development of trust and confidence between those of us representing the administration and those working on the Hill or in the departments and agencies was very important. My memory may be faulty after all these years, and we may very well have had lots more trouble than I am recalling, but I think the atmosphere of mutual trust and confidence greatly contributed to our successes.

Harold Smith's directorship is often referred to as the "golden years" of the Budget Bureau, and rightly so. I left the federal service before the many metamorphoses of the Bureau turned it into what it has since become. Those earlier years provided rewarding experiences for all of us involved. We had the sense of satisfaction that comes from knowing a job that needed to be done was getting done.

QUESTION: Do you think there is any possibility that a rational and effective approach could be adopted for selecting personnel, particularly when there is a change of administration, rather than allowing it to become the politicized and superficial approach we've seen in most administrations since the war?

MR. YOUNG: I don't know that I can answer that from my experience with any degree of authority. You're speaking primarily now of the presidential appointees?

COMMENT: Broadly.

MR. YOUNG: There has been, of course, a great proliferation in the number of appointed positions throughout the government, even below the Cabinet level. My impression is that, almost without exception, every new administration comes into office feeling it has to reinvent the wheel. One of the regrettable aspects of our system of election and the politicization of the higher echelon of appointees is the limitation on institutional memory. With the numerous changes in administrations, the institutional memory in most departments and agencies is very poor. I've often wished we had in our system something analogous to the British permanent secretaries.

But to come back to your question of whether there is a rational way for influencing this, it's perfectly natural, I think, for any new administration to want to have a cadre of senior officials that know and understand the agenda on which that administration feels it was elected. What we might deplore is the fact that consideration of ideological and political loyalty has taken priority in altogether too many instances over the examination of such personal qualifications as experience, interest, and training for the particular jobs that have to be done in the federal government. I don't see any hope for a rational approach to that without a commitment on the part of the president-elect. If there is a commitment on the part of the president-elect, and if he surrounds himself with head hunters for these governmental positions who understand that he has that goal in mind, then it is surely all right to select personnel on the basis of reasonable affinity to the president's program. None of us would object to the right of a president to appoint people who understand and want to carry out his objectives.

QUESTION: How far below all the Cabinet positions do you go before you hit the top layer of the civil service? Ken spoke about the first 1,000. In the Department of Commerce, for example, what is the level at which an incoming president cannot make appointments?

MR. YOUNG: Somebody who knows the current federal government better than I do really should answer that. My impression is that you certainly go through all the levels of assistant secretaries and their equivalents in the independent agencies. And you probably go at least one echelon below the assistant secretaries.

**COMMENT:** It varies from agency to agency. In total there are about 3,000 appointees. I once heard Bob Strauss say that if he were given permission to fill 500 positions, he could get control of an administration. So there are about 500 appointees that are very important. In addition, all the department heads have authority to make their own political appointments. They are not presidential, although they usually clear them with the White House.

There is a lot of variation and quite a few appointees who have in fact had civil service experience, even today. The most crucial place, I think, in the whole government, is the agency that you were part of, the Office of Management and the Budget. From the time you were there through 1970, no more than four people changed in the Bureau of the Budget, and usually only two—the director and the assistant director. Now, the last I counted, there were sixteen outright political appointees in the OMB, and most of the others, down to the middle-level professionals, had to be Republican and preferably supportive of Reagan before he was elected in 1980.

You spoke about institutional memory. The only place that has institutional memory in the whole government is the OMB, and even that is practically gone. This is serious. When we get a new president next year, he is going to inherit an OMB that has become almost a political office of the president, and this is supposed to be the managing agency of the federal government. I think we are really going to suffer from this.

**MR. YOUNG:** I would agree with this. It seems to me that the transition is going to be a very difficult one. But again it seems to me it will depend so much on what the president-elect establishes as his own goals in these matters and how his transition team is set up to carry out those goals.

Your mention of the significant role of the Bureau of the Budget prompts me to comment on what I think has been a very important change in the necessary priorities, if you will, of the Bureau. When the Brownlow Committee made its recommendations they were deliberately focusing upon the role of the president as the executive manager of the federal establishment. And the Bureau was conceived very much in terms of being the management arm of the president.

With the passage of time and changing economic conditions, matters of fiscal and economic policy have become paramount in the considerations concerning the operation of the Budget Bureau. These terribly important fiscal and economic matters that enter into the development of the annual budget may have pushed the management and administrative functions into a subordinate role. Is there anything to that concept of the Bureau's evolution?

COMMENT: I still think there is a good deal of review and looking into details. The management function as such has become fairly negative. They still handle things like allowances for employees overseas. They have been very big recently on collecting claims and bad debts. But as far as positive management goes, it is pretty much off the board. But on the budget they are still working on both big figures and a lot of details.

QUESTION: Isn't it true, though, that the budget has not been used by Congress through the whole Reagan administration? They may have referred to it but they haven't tried to live with any budget that has been developed by the presidential office or the Office of the Budget. Is that true or not?

COMMENT: Usually the Congress has worked from the President's budget, except for two years. They made a lot of changes. But the documents that go with the budget are very detailed. The documents for one department would fill about three file cases. It doesn't get in the newspapers and it doesn't get studied by Congress, although some of the staff work with some of it. So I wouldn't say that it was just Congress.

MR. YOUNG: I'd like to raise the question of whether anyone in this group sees any prospect for an evolution toward smaller numbers of people and greater simplicity of operation. I think much of the administrative mess has grown out of the sheer size and uncontrollability of the executive office, as well as the rivalry for turf that goes on

114

within the office. It seems to me, and I may be nostalgic, that the smoother operation of government in the old days depended very much on the smaller number of people who had to be involved. I grant that the government is larger and the nation's economy is enormously more complex in the 1980s than it was in the 1930s and 1940s. Still, I have the feeling that somehow or other, the burgeoning of numbers and the complexity of our administration exceed what is actually needed.

**COMMENT:** An analogy is the change in a business' structure as it grows from a small hands-on operation into a large multinational corporation. There, the survival of the business will depend on the changeover and putting into effect of realistic and effective management. The trouble is that we have a federal government that is going to stay in business regardless of how it responds. You had this kind of growth in complexity over the last twenty-five to fifty years, but we are still operating under the old administrative framework. In many cases, we still have the same names for a structure that we had fifty years, ago while all the problems it must deal with are different. I think the rigidities of the system are part of the problem. Each administration has tried to solve the problem by hiring more people and setting up more committees without really being able to address the central problem, namely, that the whole management structure may need a radical revision.

**MR. YOUNG:** My wife and I have done some reading recently in a book by John Colville called *The Fringes of Power*. Colville served as private secretary for Chamberlain and Churchill for about twenty years. His diary is very revealing as to the importance of continuity and how it is ensured by the private secretaries in 10 Downing Street. I don't think we have any comparable continuity in the top management of our federal government.

**NARRATOR:** The whole topic of permanent secretaries came up in connection with the anniversary of the Brownlow Commission and our transition commission. Resistance to having a permanent secretary as a link from one administration to another came from fears that too much

115

political action and too many decisions made from one side would become known to the opposition. Ted Sorensen was the leading opponent of it. In other words, a permanent secretary wouldn't be able to protect political secrets. So they pulled back.

MR. YOUNG: We've had two administrations that came into power by campaigning against the government establishment. If we get an administration that comes in with some degree of confidence in the government establishment, then you may find a little bit greater reliance on the nonpolitical leadership of the government establishment.

QUESTION: Isn't it true that, as you enlarge this political group at the top, you make it harder and harder to maintain continuity because you have a situation where the incoming man wants to get rid of everybody down to level twelve?

QUESTION: Isn't there another aspect to this? In reality, as long as you draw your top political leadership from people with relatively limited experience in the national government—and the two you were speaking of were both state governors—they are probably going to operate a good bit of the time against Washington. The British system, on the other hand, usually draws its political leadership from people who have been in Parliament for quite some time and have perhaps even been members of the Cabinet. Thus there is a body of national experience and institutional memory within the opposition. You tend not to run against the government quite as much as you might here.

Obviously, the further down we politicize the civil service, the less continuity we will have and the harder it will be to have the networks that you had when you were in government. It seems to me that we have to reassess the system of choosing our political leadership if we are to get the kind of confidence in the civil service we all hope for.

MR. YOUNG: I would agree with that point. I certainly do not want to leave the impression that I'm thinking we can achieve progress by returning to something that worked forty years ago. I think we have to start from where we are now. Whatever progress we may hope to achieve has to begin with current conditions and evolve out of that. We may learn a few helpful things from successful experiences in the past, but we certainly cannot return to the patterns that we thought worked with perfection a number of years ago.

QUESTION: Your experience in personnel management, I gather, was confined pretty much to the selection of higher level people in the new Bureau of the Budget. Is that correct?

MR. YOUNG: Not necessarily so. When I dealt with the Civil Service Commission on behalf of the Bureau, we had to deal with policies that affected the complete hierarchy, from entry levels to the top grades. A great deal of time and attention was focused on the higher echelons of the civil service, simply because it was at those levels that we were hoping to make a contribution to better management in the federal service.

COMMENT: That was the point of my question because I think there is a considerable difference between recruiting workers and managers. In the context of what I just asked, what was the nature of the tests and interviews you would apply to higher level entrants? It's hard for me to imagine such a test because I think that the only indication of ability is experience.

MR. YOUNG: I would agree with your observation. I don't have in my own files any records of what specific questions we did ask in those examinations. I think what we did for the higher echelon positions was to pose some hypothetical situations and to seek responses from the candidates as to how they might deal with them. In the personal interviews, I'm sure we tried to encourage the interviewing panel to try to assess the candidate's attitudes and "people skills." The role of an administrator or manager, after all, is perhaps nine-tenths leading other people. We would be trying to ferret out indications of whether a candidate had those abilities and qualities that lead to effective human relationships.

117

**COMMENT:** This process, in turn, relies heavily upon the ability and skill, judgments and criteria of the examiners themselves.

**MR. YOUNG:** Exactly.

**QUESTION:** What would you think of a basic examination in such subjects as geography and history and the basic sciences? It seems to me we have an awful lot of people in very high places who don't have much knowledge of these subjects.

**MR. YOUNG:** In general, I wish that our educational system produced people with a greater general knowledge of that type. There is no question that basic information of that type, and the ability to react in terms of that knowledge to specific developments, issues and problems is very necessary. I don't know whether that should become a very high priority element. If it were a high priority element, it would become almost a rejection item in the selection process.

**QUESTION:** Isn't it true that for most of the upper level positions the process was actually called the "unassembled exam" because you simply evaluated the experience record that was submitted, and that was the basic examination?

**MR. YOUNG:** Yes, this played a sizeable part in it.

**COMMENT:** And General Grant might not have passed the test?

**MR. YOUNG:** He probably could have passed the geography part of it!

**COMMENT:** A while ago we were talking about the proliferation of political appointees in the top-heavy White House and executive offices. It occurred to me that, in a certain way, we've been undone by the well-meaning writings of academics whose theorizing has now been over-simplified and reduced to folklore on the part of a generation of people coming into Washington. After World War II we began to tear down the notion that there is no difference between politics and administration. Well, if there isn't any difference, then there is no legitimate basis for reserving places for your career people, and why not let the president appoint all the people he wants to? Then in the public administration classes, instead of talking about management, we started talking about bureaucracy, the need to control it, its expansionist and imperialistic tendencies and the way it stultifies individuals. And so we arrived at another rationale for an incoming administration: the need to bring in plenty of people who can control the bureaucracy. Now we've gotten to the point where some revisionist scholars are suggesting that the whole field of public administration has been chasing a myth. It was kind of ironic that last fall the National Academy of Public Administration awarded the Brownlow Prize to a book which purportedly showed that Brownlow and all related efforts to reorganize the federal government were built on a false premise of what the presidency is and can become. So we've somehow got to evolve some new basic doctrine about the presidency and public administration and get it into operation, which I suppose will take another generation.

**MR. YOUNG:** It will.

**NARRATOR:** Maybe that is a sobering and challenging note on which to end. How many used to read Klutz' columns during World War II? I remember them as a student and a GI. There was something inspiring about them, and I wonder whether this didn't help to build public service morale, and a certain notion of the way things were done. If you happened to get stuck in Washington on the way to reassignment, you always picked up the paper and read him. Maybe that's one thing we are missing in government officials today.

At any rate, we are very grateful to you, Ed, and we certainly hope you will come back and talk again. You generated a lot of interest.

**MR. YOUNG:** I appreciate the opportunity to be with you.

# VII. One Secretary of State at a Time: Avoiding Another Irangate

## CECIL V. CRABB, JR.

**MR. MCCLESKEY:** Let me welcome you to this address. It is made possible by the generosity of the Thomas Jefferson Memorial Foundation and the Miller Center and its director Ken Thompson.

Jefferson wore many hats, but certainly his part in the conduct of foreign affairs was one of his most important roles and one in which he made a very significant contribution.

To introduce our speaker I am very pleased and honored to introduce Professor Inis Claude, who is one of the outstanding members of this department in the field of international relations. It seems appropriate to me to ask Professor Claude to make this introduction. Our speaker and he are old friends, having worked in the same vineyard. Professor Claude.

**PROFESSOR CLAUDE:** Thank you very much, Clifton. It gives me pleasure to welcome my friend Cecil Van Meter Crabb, Jr. It is eminently fitting that this lectureship should be named in honor of the man who is not only the founder of this university, but also the first secretary of state of the United States, and one of our earliest prominent ambassadors. A discussion of foreign policy under the name of Thomas Jefferson makes a great deal of sense.

Our choice of lecturer also makes a great deal of sense. Mr. Crabb spent his boyhood in Mississippi and Kentucky; he began his education at Centre College in Kentucky. Later he did a master's degree at Vanderbilt

University and completed a doctorate at Johns Hopkins University. He has spent his academic teaching career primarily at two institutions of higher learning: Vassar College from 1952 to 1968, and in the last twenty years at Louisiana State University. Along the way, he has had visiting professorships and visiting lectureships at various other places. He served a term as department chairman, both at Vassar and at LSU.

He is a distinguished teacher and research scholar in the general field of international relations, and more specifically in the area of American foreign policy. He published a book on nonalignment in the contemporary world with the intriguing title, *The Elephants and the Grass*. He has a large number of books and articles that constitute a veritable treasury of wisdom and insight on the problems and the management of American foreign policy. He has written books on the theories of American foreign relations, doctrines that are dominant in American foreign policy, the role of the president in foreign policy-making, the pragmatic approach to foreign policy-making by the United States, and so forth. I think he has a great deal to tell us about how the United States has conceived, and now conceives, its role in world affairs, and how it plays and fails to play its role in the world.

His topic for today is "One Secretary of State at a Time: Avoiding Another Irangate."

**PROFESSOR CRABB:** President Washington said on one occasion, "The United States ought to have the most successful foreign policy of any country in the world because it has so many secretaries of state." I'm sure Secretary of State Jefferson would have understood exactly what he was talking about. The problem with which we shall deal is a very old one.

Former Secretary of State Alexander Haig has said that Americans have tended to be indifferent to the utility of military power in preventing war, relying upon it only after diplomacy has failed to solve controversies with other nations. This, of course, is another way of stating Clausewitz's well-known and widely quoted dictum that war is the continuation of diplomacy or politics by other means. With national military expenditures currently running some

Cecil V. Crabb, Jr.

$300 billion annually, Americans possess a powerful military establishment. Yet Americans exhibit continued bewilderment and uncertainty about how to use force in pursuit of their national goals. For over forty years, the nation has sought to find some formula, mechanism, or process that will blend military and civilian components of national policy into an integrated whole. Recent events, and I refer specifically to what is often called "Irangate," indicate that the search must continue.

This search began in earnest at the end of World War II, owing to a combination of several factors. By way of quick review, there was the general lack of preparedness of the nation during the 1930s, which unquestionably contributed to the Japanese attack on Pearl Harbor. There was the lack of official and public understanding of the role of military force in diplomatic decision-making, as illustrated by the celebrated Stimson Doctrine (1932). There were the growing number of agencies that played a role in the foreign policy process during the New Deal. There were a number of wartime decisions, often called "military" decisions, that had far-reaching political consequences, such as the Soviet occupation of Eastern Europe, the division of Germany and Berlin, and the division of Korea and of Indochina. There was the highly personal nature of government-wide coordination of national security policy by President Roosevelt himself. As often as not, in fact, there was no coordination of such policies. And there was the example of extreme disunity within the government in the early months of the Truman administration. Finally, there was the emergence of the Cold War—a condition of no war, no peace, and the adoption of the containment policy.

Within a year or so after the end of World War II, the armed forces of the United States were reduced from some 12 million to approximately 1.6 million troops. President Truman confronted the most powerful lobby in our system, and it is not the lobby that you might expect. I refer to the "mother/wife lobby," which insisted upon bringing the boys home. The Truman White House was simply unable to resist the entreaties of that group.

After many months of study and planning under the Truman administration, the National Security Act of 1947 was enacted. As finally adopted, this act emerged as a

123

compromise among highly divergent and strongly held viewpoints within the government and throughout the nation. A new Department of Defense was created, headed by a single civilian secretary appointed by the president, yet the separate identities of the armed forces were preserved. Each armed force continued to be headed by a civilian secretary, with its own separate military commander.

A new national military strategy board, the Joint Chiefs of Staff (JCS), was established consisting of the military commanders of each of the services, with the chairman of the JCS appointed by the president. A new Central Intelligence Agency, otherwise known as the CIA, was created to provide government-wide coordination for intelligence activities.

And perhaps the body which is most directly relevant to our topic, the National Security Council (NSC), was set up with responsibility to blend military and civilian components of policy into something now called "national security policy." The National Security Council had characteristics which we should briefly note. Its membership has varied somewhat since 1947. Currently, the statutory members are the president who serves as chairman, the vice president, the secretary of state, and the secretary of defense. Other officials may be, and routinely are, invited by the president to attend NSC meetings. The NSC was placed in the Executive Office of the President, thus recognizing the preeminent role of the president in preserving national security and as guarantor of the nation's security. In effect this act codified Clinton Rossiter's description of the president as the defender of the free world.

The National Security Council is *advisory*; I do want to emphasize that word because sometimes there is misunderstanding about it. The NSC is advisory to the president. All presidents have a long list of advisers, formal and informal, whose viewpoints they may accept or reject in reaching their decisions. The president of the United States convenes the meetings of the National Security Council, determines the agenda, invites others to attend NSC meetings, and determines the purpose and the ultimate influence of NSC deliberations. As the Tower

Commission found in its recent study, only the president can make the NSC machinery work properly and effectively.

In the course of time another position was created as part of this whole machinery, called the assistant for national security affairs (ANSA). The staff and much of the work of the National Security Council are directed by the president's assistant for national security affairs. The ANSA is not a member of the National Security Council; we must bear that in mind at all times. The creation of this position dates from the Eisenhower administration in 1953. The importance and role of ANSA, as we shall see, has varied widely from one administration to the next. The performance of various incumbents in the position has been described as ranging from brilliant to disastrous.

A third component in the process is the National Security Council's staff. The National Security Act of 1947 authorized a small staff, headed by an executive secretary, appointed by the president. This staff was greatly expanded by Eisenhower. It was reduced before he left office and was reduced even further under President Kennedy and President Johnson. Under Nixon the staff grew to some fifty members in 1970. Under Carter the staff was cut back again. The purpose, role, and activities of the staff have varied considerably during the past forty years.

My colleague, Dr. Kevin V. Mulcahy, and I have identified five patterns or models of national security decision-making in the postwar period. I want to present these models as background for the discussion of Irangate.

The Truman period illustrates what we call the assistant to the president as "clerk." The National Security Council was established under the Truman administration and it began to take on at least some of its current form at that time. President Truman had very little formal training and preparation for the job. Yet his awareness at all times of the president's constitutional obligations and duties in the foreign policy field was quite remarkable. Truman also had a recollection of what one author calls the "administrative chaos" of the Roosevelt period, a situation induced deliberately in part by FDR's policies. Truman also had a great admiration for General Marshall. As wartime Chief of Staff and later as secretary of state, General Marshall was the role model for President Truman, for

Secretary of State Acheson, for Secretary of State Rusk, and for other officials in the government. Under General Marshall, very clear lines of authority existed, clear decisions were reached, and they were communicated to the President.

By contrast, Truman's early tribulations with Secretary of State James Byrnes and Secretary of Commerce Henry Wallace are well known. This period is where the phrase about multiple secretaries of state comes from, which Professor Claude quoted. After Senator Arthur H. Vandenberg informed President Truman back in 1946 that Republicans wanted a bipartisan foreign policy, but they could only deal "with one secretary of state at a time," President Truman promptly relieved Commerce Secretary Henry Wallace of his position.

Truman's administrative style, which always affects the question we are examining, was extremely interesting. On the one hand he was a humble individual. When somebody asked President Truman what was the first thing he did when he got back to Independence, Missouri after he left the White House, he replied, "I carried the suitcases up to the attic." Although Truman was a humble individual, at the same time he was a very decisive one, and forceful in his decision-making. He was determined to act when necessary, to make required decisions, and he disliked what somebody called "decision-making by exhaustion." Truman wanted a reasonable discussion of the issue, but then he wanted a decision to be reached.

Truman also was very determined—every president of course says this, but Truman was one of the few in the postwar period who really carried it out—that his secretary of state would in fact be in charge of American foreign policy under the president's direction. President Reagan said it, for example, with regard to Alexander Haig, but Truman actually meant it.

On the other hand, Truman was also suspicious of the new National Security Council machinery. He feared it might be a congressionally-instigated effort to weaken the president's authority in the foreign policy field. Alternatively, he was afraid that the NSC might become a kind of super Cabinet, as in Britain, which again might infringe upon the president's ultimate authority. Consequently, until the Korean War, the National Security Council remained at the periphery of decision-making. In contrast to Eisenhower, Truman was also unwilling to give the NSC any real responsibility for policy implementation. Truman had two appointees in the position of assistant to the president for national security. We are going to concentrate, in the interest of time, on only one: Admiral Sidney W. Souers, the first incumbent, who was called special assistant to the president for intelligence.

Admiral Souers has been described as a "shadowy figure" in the Truman White House, a model of restraint who exhibited the legendary passion for anonymity. He was lacking in overt bureaucratic or political ambitions. Admiral Souers was a quiet manager and a skilled facilitator of policy. He had wide contacts throughout the government, which he used very skillfully to achieve compromise among differing positions in the executive branch. Admiral Souers believed strongly in the primacy of the State Department in the foreign policy field, and he was careful not to create some kind of agency or operation which competed with it. He was also careful to avoid using his position to undertake independent policy initiatives or to press his own views upon the president. Under Truman, the National Security Council avoided what Dean Acheson later called the "illusion of policy" or the idea that somehow it made policy in the national security field.

The second model we have identified is the one which emerged under Eisenhower, and we call it ANSA as a "coordinator." Significant changes were made in the machinery of national security policy-making in the Eisenhower period, and the position of ANSA similarly evolved.

As a president, Eisenhower had a better-than-average background in preparation in national security and foreign affairs, perhaps better even than he realized. He assumed office at a time of very deep partisan divisions over foreign policy questions: the McCarthy era and the debate over the Korean War. Eisenhower believed that the United States needed a national strategy for waging the Cold War in which every agency of the government would participate and play an appropriate part, so that all government activities would be coordinated into a meaningful and effective whole.

127

Ike never doubted who would serve as his secretary of state. He believed, and he said, that John Foster Dulles was the best prepared individual in the history of the United States to be secretary of state. Eisenhower was extremely deferential to Dulles, giving him wide latitude. For many years, the popular impression of Eisenhower as president was of a chief executive who was ignorant of facts and events. Recently, certain revisionist works, and I refer particularly to the book by Fred Greenstein, have challenged that view. Greenstein refers to the Eisenhower adminis-tration as a period of the "hidden hand presidency." According to Greenstein, Ike in fact maintained very firm control over national policy, without appearing to do so. This approach was Eisenhower's deliberate and calculated administrative strategy.

Under Eisenhower, Republican campaign rhetoric emphasized the "New Look" in defense, cheaper defense by relying upon nuclear weapons and Dulles' idea of brinkmanship. However, during most of Ike's presidency the United States managed to avoid direct involvement in crises overseas. In spite of such GOP rhetoric, Eisenhower and Dulles basically maintained the continuity of U.S. foreign policy. Like Truman, Ike also believed that foreign affairs should be managed by the State Department—or, more precisely, by the secretary of state. It is questionable whether Dulles thought foreign affairs should be managed by the State Department, since he assumed personal charge of most policy problems.

Under Eisenhower, reliance upon the National Security Council in the national security field increased significantly. The NSC acquired new functions and greater influence; the frequency of meetings increased to about double the number that had occurred under Truman. Given his military background, Eisenhower of course was very staff-oriented; he relied heavily upon advisers, formal as well as informal. Yet Eisenhower also insisted that the NSC was advisory to the president. It did not make national policy. Secretary of State John Foster Dulles unquestionably remained the single most influential foreign policy adviser as long as he lived. Ike also relied upon the Cabinet for advice, but mainly as a device for modifying departmental compromises. Under Eisenhower, the national security staff did acquire new functions. Eisenhower had three national security advisers: Robert Cutler, Dillon Anderson and Gordon Gray. We shall concentrate briefly on Robert Cutler's career as ANSA.

Cutler was largely responsible for creating what came to be called the "policy hill." The idea was that the National Security Council would be involved in "uphill" process, in the planning and the formulation of national policy; and then it would also be involved—and this was a real innovation—in the "downhill" implementation of policy.

Under Eisenhower and Dulles, ANSA served primarily as a policy facilitator, not as an independent advocate or proponent. Eisenhower did retain and exercise ultimate power of decision-making in the national security policy field. By the end of the 1950s, as a result of its investigation, the Jackson subcommittee of Congress criticized the national security machinery that had evolved during the 1950s, on the grounds that it had become too cumbersome and bureaucratic, and that it exhibited a tendency to arrive at "least common denominator" policies.

The third model is ANSA as "advocate,"—a reference to the Kennedy-Johnson period. For the sake of brevity in our discussion we shall treat these two presidencies together.

After the Bay of Pigs fiasco, President Kennedy became very distrustful of his military and intelligence advisers. Therefore, he was inclined to make major decisions himself and to rely much more heavily upon informal advisory mechanisms. Thereafter, Kennedy, and to a lesser degree President Johnson, exhibited a deep skepticism toward the State Department. JFK viewed it as an established bureaucracy, wedded to its traditional practices and routines, and incapable of producing the kind of new ideas and proposals that the New Frontier demanded. President Johnson exhibited the typical populist distrust of the State Department, which to his mind had long been dominated by the Eastern establishment.

The era of the 1960s was one of greater-than-average military conflict and involvement by the United States. We think immediately of the Vietnam War, but also recall the Dominican intervention of 1968 and the Middle East conflict of 1967. President Kennedy preferred meeting with individual members of the National Security Council rather than holding formal sessions. The number of such sessions declined under President Kennedy. Johnson preferred what was called the "Tuesday Lunch Group," which was a collection of trusted and valued advisers. Most of the actors in the foreign policy process are agreed that the decisions of this group usually became the foreign policy decisions of the Johnson administration. More than any other chief executive since World War II, Johnson valued consensus among his advisers. Conversely, he did not encourage dissent and conflicting viewpoints. In Johnson's case, precisely how the president arrived at a decision was always a mystery to his closest advisers.

Under JFK, McGeorge Bundy served initially in the position of ANSA. He was appointed by President Kennedy and continued under President Johnson, serving from 1960 until 1966. W.W. Rostow succeeded Bundy in 1966 and served until the expiration of the Johnson administration's term.

President Kennedy accepted the recommendations of the Jackson subcommittee to scale down the size of the NSC staff. It was no longer made responsible for policy implementation. Bundy abolished the complex interagency committee structure which had been inherited from the Eisenhower White House. Under Bundy, the staff consisted of a small number of policy activists, who had no loyalty to the established departments, but were intensely loyal to the President. They were determined to bring a presidential perspective to bear upon the formulation of national security policy. In Bundy's view, the task of this staff was to seek out issues and problems, to challenge accepted wisdom on the part of established departments, to formulate policy alternatives for the President, and once the President had made up his mind, to insist upon effective implementation by the departments concerned.

The NSC staff began to hold the State Department responsible for a high level of performance. Another Bundy innovation, which by the way still exists, was the establishment of the White House situation room, a modern communication center giving the president and his staff independent access at all times to intelligence data and reports coming into executive agencies. As ANSA, Bundy acquired a reputation as a skilled facilitator and a pragmatic

Cecil V. Crabb, Jr.

problem-solver. Under both Presidents Kennedy and Johnson, the formal NSC structure was used relatively infrequently. Its primary purpose appears to have been to inform the members about decisions already reached or impending. According to George Ball, this gave the NSC the illusion of participation in the process of decision-making.

Under Kennedy and Johnson, ANSA served as a "policy advocate." He did not hesitate to evaluate departmental proposals and to give his own independent assessment to the president. In effect, Bundy and Rostow functioned as Cabinet officers.

Bundy achieved another highly influential prerogative for ANSA: direct access or physical proximity to the Oval Office. By moving his office from the Executive Office Building to the West Wing, Bundy had access to the Oval Office without an appointment or an agenda. With both Bundy and Rostow, the National Security Council staff became a source of new and creative ideas for the White House. Both of these individuals tended to serve as resident intellectuals and to provide links with the larger intellectual community.

And yet ironically, in view of the preoccupation with consensus in the Johnson period, the 1960s proved to be one of the most divisive in the diplomatic history of the United States. Again, for all of NSC's emphasis upon clarifying and providing the President with a set of policy options during the Vietnam War, in reality only a limited number of such options were in fact considered by the White House. What one student calls "Groupthink" ensued. From the results achieved during the 1960s, it seems evident that policy-makers still had not found the key to the relationship between force and diplomacy. The goal of a unified or an integrated national security policy remained an illusive undertaking.

A fourth model is illustrated by the experience of the Nixon administration, which of course came to a somewhat notorious end because of the Watergate episode. We have labelled this model ANSA as "agent" in the Nixon-Kissinger era. The Nixon presidency was a crucial stage in the evolution of the structure of the national security machinery, quite possibly the most momentous stage since 1947. By many criteria, ANSA achieved the apex of power and influence upon the course of national security policy during the early 1970s.

According to some standards, President Nixon was the best prepared occupant of the White House since World War II in terms of background in foreign affairs. Nixon obviously liked foreign affairs; he still does, as indicated by his numerous publications on the subject. He injected himself actively into external decision-making. Moreover, Nixon had a reasonably clear conception of the principles by which he expected to chart the nation's course after the Vietnam War. In the post-Vietnam War era he believed that fundamental changes were required in the nation's approach to foreign policy challenges, most of which came to be embodied in what has been called the "Nixon Doctrine."

Nixon selected Henry Kissinger to serve as ANSA for the avowed purpose of keeping control of external policy in the White House. For example, Nixon chose William Rogers as secretary of state precisely because he wanted a weak manager of the State Department. Both Nixon and Kissinger were extremely skeptical about the State Department, believing it incapable of the kind of diplomatic innovation and leadership needed in the period after the Vietnam War. Both also questioned its ideological orientation and reliability. Kissinger believed the State Department was suited only for what he somewhat derisively called "administering" foreign policy, which of course had been formulated by others, namely, the President and himself. Accordingly, the State Department was largely relegated to the periphery of the policy formulation process during the Nixon period.

Kissinger engineered the creation of a rival State Department in the White House but with President Nixon's *full concurrence and approval.* Nixon preferred to deal one-on-one with his advisers, primarily Kissinger, and others whom he could trust. The President and Kissinger often relied upon back channels, that is, dealing with foreign officials in the "situation room" and other recesses of the White House. While Nixon leaned heavily upon Kissinger in his role as ANSA, by contrast Nixon seldom utilized the formal NSC structure for advice.

As ANSA, Kissinger was determined to give Nixon the resources which he needed to exert true presidential control over the foreign policy process, including control over an unsympathetic State Department, which was regarded as long dominated by Eastern liberal thinking. Kissinger believed himself to be, and he probably was, the best prepared individual to serve in the position of ANSA since 1947. He divided the staff of the National Security Council into regional and functional units, parallel to similar units within the State Department. In effect, Kissinger exercised what one commentator has called "plenipotentiary powers." He became the symbol, the articulator, the defender, and the spokesman for President Nixon's foreign policy. In practice, Kissinger played a decisive role on three levels: policy formulation (as in the Nixon Doctrine and President Nixon's opening to China), policy implementation, and policy articulation.

Under Kissinger, ANSA functioned as a "policy agent" or, again, as a kind of British-style foreign secretary, or first secretary. Kissinger was not only equal to Cabinet members, but he appeared in some respects even to outrank them. And yet it must be emphasized that then and down to the present time, the incumbent of this position is not confirmed in the position by the Senate.

ANSA achieved the apex of its power in the Nixon-Kissinger era. Successors in the office thereafter sometimes attempted to become "another Kissinger," although none truly succeeded. Kissinger served as a kind of Cardinal Richelieu of American foreign policy. His role as policy agent, we reiterate, was played with President Nixon's full support and encouragement. No usurpation of presidential power in the foreign policy field was involved here. Despite Watergate, Nixon and Kissinger succeeded in one goal: They did reorient American foreign policy in the post-Vietnam War era. Yet in later years, even Kissinger conceded that, as he conceived of the office, ANSA was too powerful and should operate with less prominence and greater anonymity.

The pattern of the Nixon-Kissinger era, interesting as it is, obviously did not bring an end to intra-executive rivalries in the national security field. Congressional disaffection with President Nixon and with Dr. Kissinger was sometimes extremely high; Congress resented the secrecy surrounding the foreign policy process during the Nixon-Kissinger period. As ANSA, Kissinger was not viewed as particularly forthcoming or cooperative with Congress. It may also be questioned whether Nixon and Kissinger succeeded in gaining greater public and congressional understanding of America's external role in post-Vietnam War foreign policy. For example, no coherent new strategy for using the nation's armed force abroad emerged.

Finally the fifth pattern—the one at the forefront of recent national concern—we call the "insurgency model." The Reagan administration and Irangate caused the attention of the American people to be focused upon national security policy as never before. No doubt many lessons will be extracted from the Irangate episode. In our classification scheme, it may be viewed as a noteworthy example of an insurgency in the formulation and implementation of national security policy. Needless to say, this model is different from others thus far identified, precisely because it is an aberration or a deviant pattern which no student of American policy would seriously recommend for adoption. Irangate is an example of the NSC system gone wrong and getting totally out of control. ANSA, along with certain other members of the NSC staff and of the executive branch, were tempted to (and in some respects did) seize control of the policy-making process to carry out their own conceptions of external policy.

As always, in this case the administrative style and operating procedures of the incumbent president had a crucial impact in determining this outcome. One commentator has said that in performing the two duties of the American chief executive—serving as head of state and as head of the government—President Reagan should be given very high marks on the former and failing marks on the latter. As another commentator expressed it, President Reagan operated as a kind of American constitutional monarch, who fancied himself above the fray and detached from the intense bureaucratic battles being waged by his subordinates.

Ronald Reagan was perhaps in many respects the least well-prepared of any postwar chief executive in the field of external policy. The same can be said about most of his principal aides, with a few exceptions (such as Robert McFarlane and Alexander Haig). As a group, they were poorly qualified and inadequately prepared in the foreign policy field to advise the President. Yet with no background or training in foreign affairs, President Reagan exhibited little discernible interest or desire to learn more about it. One commentator described President Reagan's interest in foreign relations as "stunted." Reagan, therefore, was more than ordinarily dependent upon the views and recommendations of his advisers.

In contrast to the Carter administration, however, Reagan also possessed a very strong preconception of what he wanted to do in the sphere of external policy: stand tall, make America great again, enhance respect for the nation, improve America's credibility, and actively contest communists, terrorists, and others threatening U.S. interests overseas. After becoming president, of course, he found that many of these preconceived desires were at odds with reality. Time and time again—and Soviet-American relations provided an excellent example—President Reagan was compelled to modify his rhetorical position in the light of prevailing realities.

As chief executive, Ronald Reagan has preferred to focus upon major issues and larger questions, leaving his advisers to fill in the details. Reagan believed that a preoccupation with the details of national policy had seriously weakened President Carter's position and had detracted from his diplomatic record. By contrast, Reagan conceived of his function as supplying the vision needed to achieve the nation's internal and external goals.

President Reagan never clearly designated anyone in the White House staff as his principal deputy. Throughout most of his term in office, therefore, lines of authority among his advisers were unclear and ambiguous. There was no clearly understood chain of command among the members of the presidential staff. Precisely how decisions were made or reached in the Reagan White House was never very clear. Considerable confusion and uncertainty existed even among Reagan's advisers on this point. In many instances the President's decisions were not written down or formally recorded. According to one account, Reagan sometimes approved policy recommendations submitted to the National Security Council even before they had been submitted for discussion. Reagan liked a staff consensus. When this occurred, as a rule, he approved the understanding, which then became accepted policy.

In many spheres, however, such as disarmament policy, infighting among his advisers continued up to the stage of policy implementation. At times, confused White House directives left considerable running room for Reagan's subordinates and for executive agencies. Yet when no consensus existed among his principal aides—and this appeared to have been the rule during much of Reagan's tenure in the White House—President Reagan appeared to be bewildered and uncertain as to what he ought to do about it. Reagan was disinclined to "knock heads" or otherwise compel his aides to reach agreement. As a result, he has tolerated an extraordinarily high level of dissension and disagreement over policy among his subordinates. Informal groupings existed within the executive branch, such as one called the "family group," which consisted of Secretary of State Shultz, former Secretary of Defense Weinberger, former CIA Director Casey, and Robert McFarlane, the former national security adviser. This was a kind of administrative "big four," which held private meetings in order to reach agreement and to resolve their differences.

The National Security Council under President Reagan exhibited some interesting features. A succession of individuals held the post of ANSA. For the most part these people had no formal training or preparation for the job. Many of the members of President Reagan's staff appeared to be uncertain about their duties. They had to acquire on-the-job training; in effect, they have had to write their own job descriptions. Because of a lack of training and preparation by most participants, the decision-making process in the Reagan White House became heavily weighted against making difficult decisions or taking bold steps. When they were finally reached, positions adopted by the National Security Council were frequently ambiguous and did little to end bureaucratic infighting.

Internal procedures within the National Security Council under Reagan were poorly defined and loose. For example, Admiral Poindexter said he would have approved the arms-for-hostage deal with Iran if he had been asked by Oliver North. President Reagan said he would not have given his approval, if he had been asked. Again, procedures for communicating presidential decisions were ill-defined and poorly supervised. Oliver North contended that he sent President Reagan several memoranda concerning covert aid to the Contras. His superior, Admiral Poindexter, contended these were never received. President Reagan also denied ever having seen or approved them.

Despite the celebrated Al Haig affair in the early months of the Reagan presidency, in the Reagan White House the exact scope and responsibilities of the office of secretary of state were never subsequently delineated or defined. Major questions existed concerning whether President Reagan, not to speak of his advisers, really wanted a vicar of foreign policy.

In the Reagan White House, ANSA performed a number of extremely interesting and diverse functions, as revealed by evidence disclosed by the Tower Commission Report and the congressional hearings on Irangate. These included: protecting the President from certain advisers (such as Haig), whose views were regarded as unwelcome; asserting a hardline conservative view against the pragmatists on the Reagan team; projecting a tough U.S. image overseas; and exhibiting a willingness to use force when necessary.

In some periods, the principal function of the NSC staff appeared to be preventing political damage to President Reagan. Alternatively, ANSA sometimes sought to limit the kind of public relations damage caused by former Secretary of Defense Weinberger's unpopular campaigns on Capitol Hill for higher defense spending. In addition, Robert McFarlane appeared to have devoted a considerable amount of time to keeping the peace between Weinberger and Shultz. As the Iran-Contra affair indicates, some members of the NSC staff believed that they had a unique mission: devising means for circumventing legal restrictions upon the President's diplomatic action and bypassing the expressed will of Congress. Again, from the evidence of the Iran-Contra episode, in some instances, the National Security staff assumed operational responsibilities for carrying out policies abroad.

On a different front, Robert McFarlane sometimes concentrated upon improving relations with Congress. It was said that during some periods he was the most acceptable member of the Reagan foreign policy team on

137

Capitol Hill. Moreover, McFarlane played a key role in efforts to limit the anti-communist rhetoric of certain other Reagan advisers. Other members of the NSC staff used public funds in attempts to change public attitudes and congressional viewpoints on aid to the Contras.

As ANSA, Admiral Poindexter saw his job, and these are his own words, as "protecting the President" and giving him "plausible deniability" in the scheme to provide secret aid to the Contras. On advice from Robert McFarlane, Oliver North gave political assistance in turn to the Contras on how to achieve greater internal political unity and how to adopt a common platform. One NSC staff member was sent abroad to gauge the reaction of foreign leaders and governments to President Reagan's policies toward Central America. Again, Robert McFarlane and Oliver North sought to make Contra forces militarily credible. Oliver North used funds from the arms sale to promote the political fortunes of some members of the Contra group *vis-a-vis* other members. Again, Oliver North endeavored to improve the climate of opinion in Washington for the Contra cause. He sought to get Congress to change its mind and to repeal the Boland Amendment. North also advised Contra leaders on the proper tactics to use in dealing with Congress. Led by Oliver North, the NSC staff functioned as a kind of military strategy board, advising the Contras on how to undertake successful military campaigns against the Sandinistas. On a different front, Oliver North personally negotiated with Israel to provide military advisors, captured Soviet weapons, and provided other forms of aid to the Contras. Finally—and this, of all these things on the list, intrigues me most—Oliver North personally threatened the President of Costa Rica with a cut-off of U.S. aid if he exposed covert U.S. aid to the Contras.

Let me briefly summarize some of the lessons of the Iran-Contra episode in the light of this forty-year history of the National Security Council. During this period, the NSC mechanism quite clearly has *not* succeeded in producing a unified and coherent national security policy. The goal remains elusive. The Iran-Contra affair raises anew that question from ancient times, "Who watches the watchman?" The group that is expected to unify, oversee, and monitor the activities of agencies engaged in national security policy has itself run amok, and in the process created major problems for the United States in foreign affairs.

This leads to another thought. The Iran-Contra aberration no doubt took place for many reasons. Clearly a major one was President Reagan's own detached and uninvolved approach to decision-making. Different as the presidential styles may have been in each of the models we discussed, each one presupposed that the chief executive will somewhat forcibly discharge his constitutional duties. A primary one of those duties is to "ride herd" on members of his immediate staff and to demand full and accurate reporting by his subordinates. Yet as the Tower Commission found, President Reagan did not drive the system; ANSA and subordinates within the NSC staff in effect took over the wheelhouse and navigated the ship of state, displacing the President in this role.

A related problem underscored by Irangate was the lack of clear direction in American foreign policy since the Vietnam War. As one commentator expressed it, the Reagan administration appeared to have no game plan. Under these conditions, members of the National Security staff were tempted to devise and implement their own. Oliver North and company moved to fill this vacuum in national security policy. They believed they had a coherent policy, they believed that their goals were attainable; and they were convinced that President Reagan at least tacitly approved of their activities abroad, because they were carrying out the general goals of his administration.

Finally, the Iran-Contra episode graphically calls attention to an unfortunate and recurrent reality. Time after time since World War II, officials involved in national security policy have lacked the background, expertise, and knowledge required to make sound decisions in external policy. This may well be the most fundamental reason why Irangate happened. Beginning with the President himself, and including nearly all of those individuals participating in making and implementing national security policy in the Reagan era, very few had any noteworthy training or expertise qualifying them to respond intelligently to events in the Middle East, Central America, and other regions. The Irangate episode stands as an example of uninformed people giving bad advice to a president who was even more than ordinarily dependent upon the views of his aides. We may be thankful that under these conditions the Reagan White House was not confronted with another Cuban missile crisis entailing the risk of nuclear war!

I want to close by quoting something which Dean Rusk said several years ago. He said that he would like to have the second article of the Constitution of the United States—which invests the executive power of the government in a single president—inscribed in the White House dining room, so that all the officials could see it every day and think about it. In light of Irangate, I would like to amend Secretary Rusk's motion by saying that perhaps the proper starting point for that inscription is the Oval Office itself.

QUESTION: Dr. Crabb, many scholars have noted that the Foreign Service has been under-utilized and neglected in the past thirty years. In the last year or so, or since George Shultz has been secretary of state, have we seen a good trend in this regard? Has the State Department been allowed to reassert itself in policy?

PROFESSOR CRABB: I'll be perfectly honest with you. I'm not certain at this stage whether this influence or resurgence by Secretary Shultz is very significant. It seems to me that it could be one of two things. It could be similar to the role John Foster Dulles played under President Eisenhower. In that situation the secretary of state himself was influential, but it did not mean the State Department as an institution was important. Dulles was very distrustful of the State Department. Dulles didn't do very much, in my opinion, to enhance the influence and the impact of the State Department. In fact, on the contrary, he diminished it. Or perhaps we are seeing a reversion to the style of Dean Acheson, who was very much oriented toward the State Department, who relied upon it heavily, and who used its resources. I'm not sure. I'm inclined to think it is more a reversion to the Dulles style. You may think I'm overly pessimistic and negative about this. I'm inclined to think at this point, however, that it may be closer to the Dulles style than to the Achesonian model. I think there are some real reasons why any resurgence by the State Department is going to be very difficult.

140

In regard to the resources of the Foreign Service, I agree that we have under-utilized them, and I'm mightily distressed. I fought this battle fairly recently on the LSU campus. I was absolutely dumfounded and horrified when the graduate school proposed to eliminate the language requirement for the Ph.D. degree. The last thing in the world we need in the United States is to be moving in that direction. We would already win the prize, I think, for having the poorest language facility of any nation in the world. And with the university's highest degree we are not going to require any facility in a foreign language, but we are going to leave it to departments? This means a lot of departments won't require language skills. I think that is shocking and disgraceful.

I don't know for certain what the founder of the University of Virginia would have said about this, but I doubt whether he would have accepted this change. We've been hurt by the Jacksonian conception of democracy and the glorification of the common man. Jackson said on one occasion that there was no job in the federal government that the ordinary person was not perfectly qualified to do. This sounds as though there is some kind of a conflict between a high degree of training or expertise and democracy. We have been captivated by that idea; we've been controlled by it.

QUESTION: Professor Crabb, you noted that some presidents and secretaries of state distrusted what you called the "liberal Eastern establishment," especially in the State Department. Isn't it futile and foolish for high executive officials to regard the State Department bureaucracy as an enemy to be contained or overcome?

PROFESSOR CRABB: I didn't say that fear was rational. The point is, though, in the case of the Nixon administration, that Kissinger was a Republican. In the minds of Nixon and Kissinger, the so-called Eastern establishment tends to be predominantly Democratic. How could they disassociate themselves from their own bureaucracy? You are absolutely right; they did not regard themselves as part of the establishment. And why didn't they? I don't know how they got by with that act! It was

141

pretty skillful: They did it on the grounds that they were Republican and they claimed the Eastern establishment reflected liberal, Democratic ideas. They thought that they were there to correct past errors and that in the past the State Department had been misguided.

Perhaps part of this goes back to the McCarthy period and the fears expressed then about the State Department being under left-wing influence. After all, remember how Richard Nixon made his political reputation. He gained national prominence as a sort of crusader against communism.

**QUESTION:** How will history ultimately judge Oliver North?

**PROFESSOR CRABB:** You know what the prophet Amos said: "I am neither a prophet nor the son of a prophet." But I will mention my personal feeling. I agree with President Lincoln that the common sense of the American people will eventually prevail. Sooner or later the American people, realizing that North was usurping power, will take a very negative view of him. It was an actual usurpation of power with no legal or constitutional basis. That's not necessarily the view at the moment. Oliver North is something of a folk hero to some people at the present time. It reminds me of what happened to General Douglas MacArthur during the Korean War. For many months, even several years, there was great popular disaffection with Truman's decision to dismiss General MacArthur. Yet over the course of time, most people came to agree with President Truman's dismissal of MacArthur. Some people wanted to impeach Truman. There was a Herblock cartoon that showed two highly indignant citizens standing on the street corner. One of them said, "Who does President Truman think he is, the president?" As time went on, common sense prevailed. I think that is going to happen sooner or later with Oliver North.

**MR. MCCLESKEY:** On behalf of the Thomas Jefferson Memorial Foundation, the Department of Government and Foreign Affairs, and the Miller Center, let me thank Professor Crabb for this extraordinary lecture.

# Concluding Observations

Inquiries into governance reflect both an ancient tradition and an emerging interest in the study of politics. Aristotle examined the distribution of power and authority within different regimes. Classical political thought was a study in the ideally best and best possible political systems. Pre-modern political thought was more inclined to focus on the whole whereas modern political thought has as its focus the study of the parts of the political system.

The revival of concern with governance reflects, it seems to me, a return to the emphasis on the whole, and more particularly, the interconnectedness of the separate branches of government which each have become the subject of highly specialized research and study. Thus the governance approach is a countertrend to the intellectual currents and dominant movements in postwar political science. Without neglecting the scientific and systematic research that has prevailed in the field, it tries to put together the many fragments of understanding and knowledge in order to better understand the whole.

The present volume is a first tentative investigation of the validity of this approach, calling as it does on authorities in different spheres of politics to look more broadly for points of intersection and interrelation among the diverse arenas of politics and governance. Because there is nothing new under the sun and because philosophy and political thought is, as Whitehead once said, a footnote to Plato, the approach of this little volume is not new. It is, however, an effort to inspire a rethinking of certain approaches to the study of the presidency and of American political institutions.